R. Chudley
FFB, MCIOB, MRSH

The maintenance and adaptation of buildings

Illustrated by the author

Longman London and New York

Longman Group Limited

Longman House
Burnt Mill, Harlow, Essex, UK

Published in the United States of America
by Longman Inc., New York

© Longman Group Limited 1981

First published 1981

British Library Cataloguing in Publication Data
Chudley, R
    The maintenance and adaptation of buildings.
    (Longman technician series: construction and
    civil engineering).
    1. Buildings — Maintenance
    2. Buildings — Remodelling for other use
    I. Title
    690'.24   TH3301   80–40142
    ISBN 0–582–41573–X

Printed in Singapore by
Kua Co., Book Manufacturer, Pte Ltd

Longman Technician Series

Construction and Civil Engineering

General Editor – Construction and Civil Engineering

C. R. Bassett, B.Sc.
*Formerly Principal Lecturer in the Department of Building and Surveying,
Guildford County College of Technology*

Books already published in this sector of the series:

Construction technology Volume 1   *R. Chudley*
Construction technology Volume 2   *R. Chudley*
Construction technology Volume 3   *R. Chudley*
Construction technology Volume 4   *R. Chudley*
Construction mathematics Volume 1   *M. K. Jones*
Construction mathematics Volume 2   *M. K. Jones*
Building services and equipment Volume 1   *F. Hall*
Building services and equipment Volume 2   *F. Hall*
Building services and equipment Volume 3   *F. Hall*
Construction science Volume 1   *B. J. Smith*
Construction science Volume 2   *B. J. Smith*
Practical construction science   *B. J. Smith*
Construction surveying   *G. A. Scott*
Materials and structures   *R. Whitlow*
Building organization and procedures   *G. Forster*

Contents

Chapter 5 Deterioration and defects 91

Chapter 6 Causes and methods of repair, renewal and alterations 108

Chapter 7 Maintenance management 141

Introduction

The main aim of this book is to provide a basic text covering the requirements of the standard unit in the maintenance and adaptation of buildings as
suggested by the appropriate Programme Committee of the Technician
Education Council.

It has been assumed that the readers to whom this book is directed have
successfully completed a Technician Education Council course of study in
construction technology to level III. It is in no way intended to be a maintenance manual for the use of craftsmen or do-it-yourself enthusiasts since the
primary objectives of the unit are to appreciate and understand the planning,
economic, legal, organization and managerial aspects of maintenance of
buildings as well as providing a general knowledge of maintaining, repairing,
and adapting buildings.

No textbook can ever give a complete and up-to-date coverage of all the
aspects of any subject, therefore students are strongly recommended to study
other sources of reference and information particularly those involving case
studies so that they may learn from the experience and mistakes of others.

Acknowledgements

We are grateful to the following for permission to reproduce copyright material:

British Standards Institution for reference to British Standards, Codes of Practice; Building Research Establishment for extracts from Building Research Establishment publications; Her Majesty's Stationery Office for extracts from Acts, Regulations and Statutory Instruments.

I should like to express my gratitude to my colleagues at the Guildford County College of Technology for their help and comments during the preparation of this book, and finally I wish to record my thanks to my wife for typing the entire manuscript.

Roy Chudley
1980

Cover photograph by Richard Costain Construction Group

Chapter 1

Principles

Before commencing a study of the maintenance and adaptation of buildings the definitions of the terms 'maintenance' and 'adaptation' should be understood.

Maintenance

This term comes from the French verb 'maintenir', which means to hold. In the context of this study it means to hold, keep, sustain or preserve the building or structure to an acceptable standard. Maintenance is therefore the act of maintaining. To many people maintenance is synonymous with repair and this is a very common misconception. In the act of maintaining repairs or indeed replacement may well be necessary but the primary objective of all maintenance procedures is to avoid as far as practicable the need to repair or replace the structure, fittings, services, equipment or furnishings which collectively make up the total environment of any building. The real problem in defining maintenance is: what is an acceptable standard? This is of course a matter of conjecture and is generally subjective: each owner or tenant will have to establish his own standards based on factors such as usage of building; anticipated life; availability of capital, materials and manpower; changes in usage and personal or business prestige. All of these factors will be examined in greater detail in subsequent chapters.

Adaptation

This term comes from the Latin *ad* (to); *aptare* (to fit) and in the context of this study adaptation means the process of adjustment and alteration of a structure or building and/or its environment to fit or suit new conditions.

It can also include the provision of extra accommodation by addition to or extension of the existing structure or building. The extent to which adaptation can be carried out is governed by factors such as planning permission, legal requirements, capital available and the availability of all forms of resources. These factors, like those given above for maintenance aspects, will be considered in greater depth in subsequent chapters.

It can be concluded from the above comments that the degree to which a structure or building is to be maintained can be influenced by many factors and if maintenance is not carried out to sustain an acceptable standard then deterioration and decay of the structure or building will take place.

Deterioration is where the condition of a structure or a building and/or its components degenerate or become worse, whereas decay of a structure or building and/or its components rot, waste away or decompose, very often to the point where replacement is the only solution. One method of planning against these forces is to appreciate the primary agents, sources and causes of deterioration and decay.

The primary agents, sources and causes of deterioration and decay in structures and buildings can be listed and briefly commented upon as follows:

1. Human.
2. Chemical.
3. Atmospheric.
4. Structural.
5. Moisture.
6. Fire.
7. Faulty design.
8. Faulty construction.
9. Faulty materials.
10. Faulty components.
11. Faulty systems.
12. Cleaning.
13. Vandalism.

1. Human: failure to clean and carry out routine maintenance; ignorance of the causes of deterioration and decay; poor planning, budgeting or allocation of monetary resources to enable maintenance activities to be financed; lack of understanding of the legal obligations, responsibility and accountability of maintenance aspects; poor security leading to vandalism; failure to promote awareness of maintenance needs by all who use the building; using temporary methods instead of adequate methods; failure to establish an acceptable standard of maintenance for the premises; adopting a negative attitude of waiting until emergency measures are required and blatant abuse of the building, its fittings, finishes and furnishings.

2. Chemical: interaction of certain cleaning agents with materials and/or components causing disintegration, softening or discoloration; activities or processes creating an internal or external climate likely to promote corrosion, deterioration and decay of materials and components and the interaction of certain dissimilar materials in close contact with one another.

3. Atmospheric: reaction of the structure, external fabric, finishes and claddings to the elements such as wind, rain, sun, frost and snow; reaction of the building to the penetration of the above elements and the reaction of the structure, external fabric, finishes and claddings to the pollution in the atmosphere.

4. Structural: settlement, moisture, shrinkage and thermal movements and the reactions of the structural elements being supported to these movements; reaction of the structural members due to changes in the loading patterns or intensities; natural ageing of the structural members; reaction to the corrosive elements in the atmosphere and internal climate and deterioration due to infrequent inspections or inadequate maintenance.

5. Moisture: penetration of the external fabric or claddings and through ground floor constructions giving rise to dampness and possibly creating the conditions suitable for fungi growth or attack; excess moisture in the internal atmosphere which could lead to excessive condensation, corrosion and possibly electrical faults.

6. Fire: aftermath of a fire leading to the complete replacement; repairs to the fabric, components, structural elements, fittings, finishes and furnishings; weakening of any part of the building not directly affected by a fire and the spoiling of fittings, furnishings, finishes and decorations caused by the fire fighters whilst bringing the outbreak under control.

7. Faulty design: poor specification of materials due to lack of knowledge of their properties and the substitution of unavailable materials or components by unsuitable replacements; insufficient finance leading to the selection of sub-standard materials and/or components; lack of adequate consideration of future maintenance problems; inadequate provisions for access to carry out maintenance activities and lack of design flexibility due to rigid constraints imposed by the client.

8. Faulty construction: lack of supervision during construction period; failure to understand or follow exactly the specification and/or drawings; failure to replace defective work; failure of designer or architect to adequately monitor works in progress; lack of skilled labour; over-emphasis on need for quantity rather than quality and the failure to fully appreciate the consequences of shoddy or poor work and/or materials.

9. Faulty materials: failure of client, builder, designer or architect to reject sub-standard materials; inadequate inspection of materials by supplier and/or receiver; provision of inadequate storage facilities on site and inadequate or inconsistent mixing of materials on site.

10. Faulty components: similar conditions to those given above for faulty materials can lead to deterioration and decay of the fabric, services or finishes of the structure or building.

11. Faulty systems: inadequate knowledge on the part of the designer or architect leading to an unsatisfactory design, detail or system; inability of the installer or builder to follow the specification and/or drawings; inadequate testing of the system before being commissioned; failure of owner to follow maintenance instructions provided by manufacturer or designer and the inability of the owner to operate the system as instructed.

12. Cleaning: failure to carry out routine cleaning operations; use of incorrect cleaning materials and/or techniques; inadequate supervision of cleaners to ensure that cleaning is thorough; failure of owner or tenant to provide sufficient space, enough time or the correct equipment and materials for cleaning operations and the failure to employ specialists for cleaning special fittings and equipment.

13. Vandalism: lack of security; failure to promote awareness among occupants of the consequences of deliberate and not deliberate vandalism; incorrect selection of materials and finishes in circulation areas which are prone to vandalism and failure to maintain or repair areas of damage caused by vandals thus encouraging more vandalism.

It must be appreciated that the causes and sources of deterioration and decay given above cannot necessarily be taken in isolation since there are generally several interacting causes and sources which promote deterioration and decay. If these causes and sources can be identified then steps can be taken during the brief, design, construction and occupation stages of build-ings to reduce the amount and need for maintenance. It is such an important aspect of the maintenance and adaptation of buildings that a separate section (Ch. 5) has been devoted to a deeper analysis and study of these aspects.

Maintenance and the Gross National Product

The Gross National Product (GNP) is a term used in economics to indicate the total market value of the goods and services produced by a nation's economy during a specific period of time, which in most cases is taken as one year. The GNP does not take into account or allow for any depreciation or consumption of the goods or services used to calculate the figure. If these are taken into account the result is known as the Net National Product (NNP).

It is never possible to give up-to-date, 100 per cent accurate figures to the part played by the maintenance and adaptation of buildings in terms of the GNP. Statistics of this magnitude take time to evaluate, the ebb and flow of the nation's economy can alter the whole spectrum in a very short space of time, there is no way of accurately knowing how much or of what nature do-it-yourself enthusiasts contribute to the GNP and monetary values have little significance due mainly to the constant trend of world inflation. It is better therefore to generalize in percentage terms, allowing for a reasonable

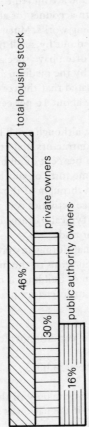

The nation's capital stock

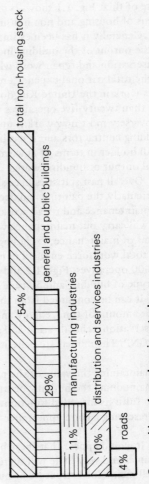

Composition of housing stock

Composition of non-housing stock

Fig. 1.1. Composition of the nation's stock in terms of value

amount of tolerance which in some circumstances can be as high as 20 per cent. If, for example, the nation's building stock is considered in relationship to other forms of the nation's stock it cannot be considered stable since new structures and buildings are being constantly added to the total and conversely subtracted from the total due to demolition works. These two facets are not necessarily in unison, therefore the actual figures are in a perpetual state of flux. Fig. 1.1 shows typical comparisons of the nation's stock in terms of housing and non-housing stock.

Generally it has been estimated that during recent years about one-fifth of the output of the building industry can be attributed to maintenance, conservation and repair work which in turn accounts for about 30 per cent of the total national expenditure on building works. Much of the maintenance work in the United Kingdom is carried out by small firms employing less than twenty-five operatives who very often have specialists' skills. Conversely most new work is undertaken by the medium and large size building contractors and it has been estimated that the contribution of the small builder in terms of new work is only about 16 per cent of the yearly total output of building works.

Overall past statistics have shown that although small building firms, particularly the painting and decorating contractors, tend to concentrate on maintenance and repair works some 85 per cent of all building contractors will carry out maintenance work in some form or another. Taking all forms of maintenance, excluding cleaning, throughout the building industry the total workforce engaged in maintenance activities is in the region of 60 000 operatives. Figs. 1.2 and 1.3 show typical patterns of maintenance by type of building and by type of craft or trade.

It can be concluded from the above that during any given period of time a fair amount of time, energy and money in terms of the maintenance, repair, conservation, rehabilitation and adaptation of buildings is contributed to the GNP. The immediate benefits of good maintenance practices are namely:

1. Maintaining the value of the property.
2. Maintaining the building or structure in a condition which will enable it to fulfil its intended function.
3. Presenting a good appearance to the general public.

It would appear that these benefits accrue mainly to the owner or occupier and very little will therefore benefit the nation as a whole, but a well-maintained structure or building will also achieve a high degree of efficiency which can in turn increase the morale of those living or working within its environment and it may also lead to an increase in productivity within manufacturing complexes.

The three benefits given above can be interrelated, one aiding the other. Morale is normally regarded as a human quality and if this is high the attitude, quality and efficiency of a person usually increases – resulting in increased production without extra effort or abnormal increased costs. Efficiency can be related to humans, services and equipment and if the

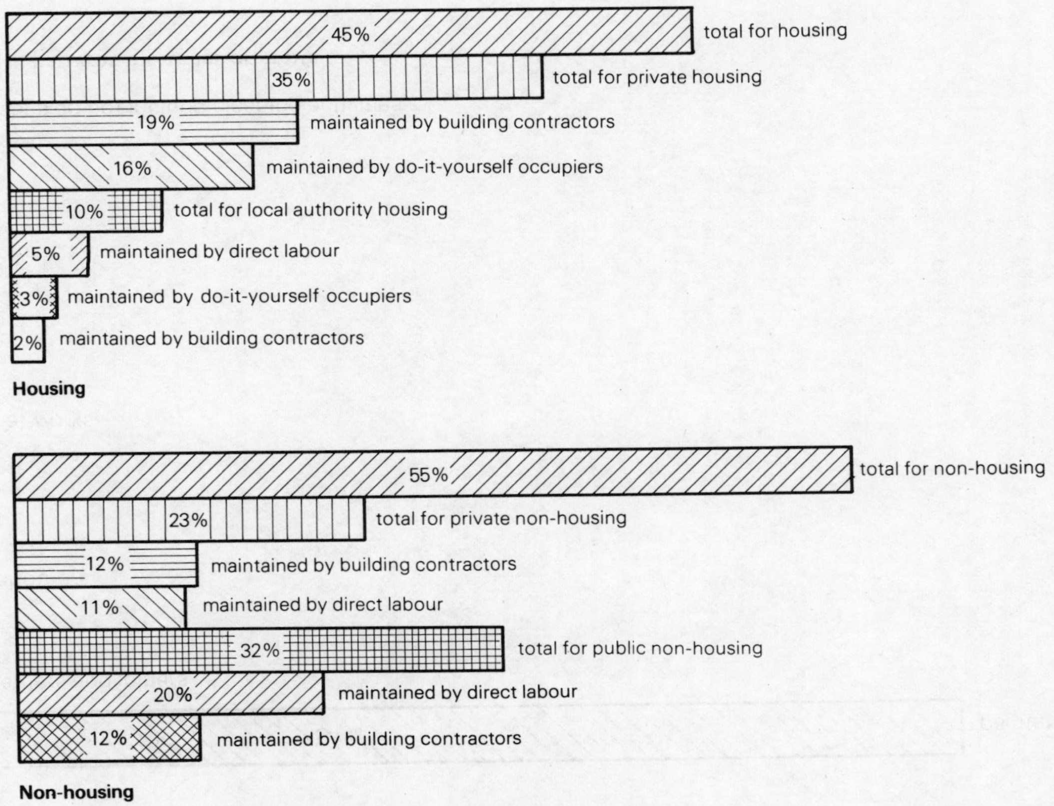

Housing

- total for housing — 45%
- total for private housing — 35%
  - maintained by building contractors — 19%
  - maintained by do-it-yourself occupiers — 16%
- total for local authority housing — 10%
  - maintained by direct labour — 5%
  - maintained by do-it-yourself occupiers — 3%
  - maintained by building contractors — 2%

Non-housing

- total for non-housing — 55%
- total for private non-housing — 23%
  - maintained by building contractors — 12%
  - maintained by direct labour — 11%
- total for public non-housing — 32%
  - maintained by direct labour — 20%
  - maintained by building contractors — 12%

Fig. 1.2. Typical maintenance patterns by building type

8

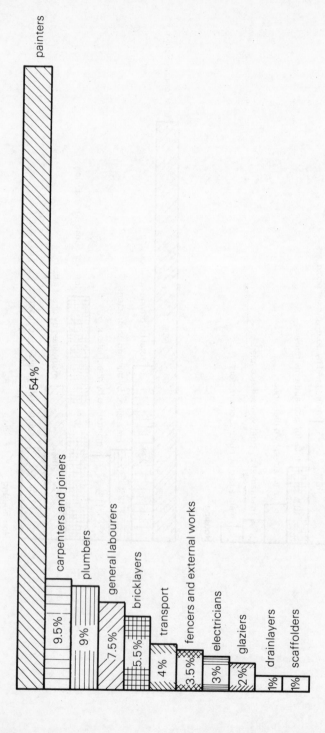

painters 54%

carpenters and joiners 9.5%

plumbers 9%

general labourers 7.5%

bricklayers 5.5%

transport 4%

fencers and external works 3.5%

electricians 3%

glaziers 2%

drainlayers 1%

scaffolders 1%

NB   The above comparisons do not include cleaning activities

Fig. 1.3. Typical maintenance patterns by trades or crafts

services and equipment are maintained to a high standard this again will instil high morale in the people using the services and equipment, so completing the cycle of better efficiency and a higher increased production which can be related to the GNP. It is therefore fair to conclude that although maintenance may not have a high direct relationship to the GNP its indirect influence can be considerable. The relationship of maintenance and the GNP is shown diagrammatically in Fig. 1.4.

Factors influencing the decision to carry out maintenance

Maintenance can be planned or unplanned; in the latter is is very often a case of taking no action until failure occurs and repair or replacement becomes a matter of urgency. This of course is not a very satisfactory state of affairs from the user's point of view or indeed from an economic aspect. The topics of economical maintenance and planned maintenance will be considered in detail in subsequent chapters of this text. It is therefore only necessary in this consideration of basic principles to look at the various factors which may influence the decision to carry out maintenance work and these factors can be listed as follows:

1. Costs
2. Age of property
3. Availability of physical resources
4. Urgency
5. Future use
6. Social considerations.

Costs

The costs of maintenance may at first sight seem to be a simple matter of how much must be expended on the material and labour contents to carry out a particular maintenance task; but before coming to a decision to implement a particular item of maintenance other cost factors must be considered. If a certain sum of money is to be expended on a maintenance item does this mean that some other form of expenditure has to be sacrificed? If this is the case, can the proposed sacrifice be justified? or is there a compromise such as short-term maintenance of lower initial cost which will suffice until sufficient funds are available for long-term maintenance to be carried out?

If the company has been prudent and set aside in its annual budget a capital sum for maintenance work, is this adequate to cover the cost of the work under consideration? If not, short-term maintenance could be considered but this in itself may be uneconomic in the long term, therefore a decision must be made as to whether further finance for immediate long-term maintenance should be arranged.

The actual costs and nature of all maintenance work should always be under constant surveillance so that budgeting for future work, the purchase

10

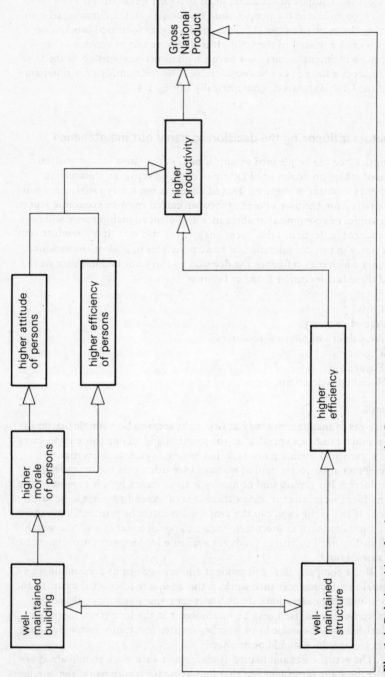

Fig. 1.4. Relationship of maintenance to the Gross National Product

of equipment, the buying of materials which can be economically held in stock, the employment of permanent labour for maintenance activities can be assessed and future trends in material and labour costs can be estimated.

Another cost aspect of maintenance work which is worthy of consideration is that of major maintenance works in conjunction with regular or cyclic maintenance items. If for example a major maintenance activity requires the use of plant such as a scaffold it may be prudent to advance the date of other works which would need the same access facilities, thus constituting a saving on the overall maintenance costs. It must be appreciated that to be viable the advanced work must be work which has been programmed for the immediate or near future, since by advancing maintenance by too great a period of time would not make full economic use of the last maintenance work which was carried out.

Age of property

All buildings and structures consist of materials and components linked together to form the desired unit of accommodation and all such materials and components will start to age from the moment they are incorporated into the building during the construction period. Indeed, many will have started to age prior to their being delivered to the building site. Collectively the individual ageing of the materials and components will age the building as a whole. The rate at which this takes place will depend on a number of factors such as the expected life of any particular material or component, its position in the building, its degree of exposure, the external or internal climatic conditions of the building, the amount of use or misuse it received and its interaction with other materials or components.

To assess the life of any particular material, component or element can be achieved by referring to manufacturers' data, research papers, feed-back information and personal experience. Any material can be classified as having reached its life expectancy when it ceases to be effective. It must be remembered that very few materials will reach their estimated life expectancy unless they have been adequately maintained during their life even if this means only periodic cleaning.

Any building, like the materials and components of which it is constructed, will also have an estimated life expectancy since as the materials and components wear out so this will lessen the overall effectiveness of the building and consequently its remaining useful life, because this is obviously limited by the amount of capital which can be expended to keep the building as an economic asset. It is very difficult to ascertain when a building has in fact reached the end of its effective life since the owner may be thinking in terms of the economic or functional life rather than the physical life. Buildings of historical or architectural interest are of course in a special category since although the maintenance costs may be very high their attraction to tourists and visitors can be of great value to the area in which the building is situated or to the nation as a whole, apart from the national pride in our heritage.

To obtain the maximum life out of materials, components, services, equipment and the building itself a planned programme of inspections and cyclic maintenance should be established as soon as the building has been handed over by the contractor or acquired from the vendor. In simple terms this means taking a complete inventory of all the materials, components, services and equipment comprising the building and assessing or estimating at what intervals inspections and routine maintenance will be required, and also estimating the amount of capital which must be allocated to cover these aspects.

Availability of physical resources

Physical resources in the context of maintenance and adaptation of buildings can be defined as all the materials, components, services and equipment which are contained in the whole of the construction and fitting out of a building, and therefore when an item of maintenance is being planned the availability of any of these physical resources must be considered.

The last section dealt with the question of age and it should by now be appreciated that many materials and components have a relatively long life and when the time comes for their replacement difficulty may be experienced in obtaining an exact match in all respects. If we take some examples from the long life materials it will be possible to illustrate the problems of availability. Lead used for flashings, gutter linings and soakers can have a life expectancy of about sixty years so that if it needs renewal there should be no problem since the material is still used throughout the industry and is readily available. If however we consider roof tiles with a life expectancy of about fifty years they may well be of a type which is no longer manufactured. If this is the case what is the answer? It may be possible to find an acceptable match in terms of constructional and aesthetical blend.

Sometimes a suitable quantity and quality may be obtained from a demolition or salvage contractor, bearing in mind that such a source of physical resources may take time in locating, and when found the material will probably be well aged and therefore provide only a short-term remedy. In such a situation it may be worth while considering replacing the whole area with new materials, thus giving the whole area a complete new lease of life, assuming that the rest of the building will justify the extra capital outlay. If the area to be replaced is small relative to the remainder it may be possible to have some 'specials' made which will blend with the original in all respects.

It is very difficult to be specific when considering a topic of this nature since each problem must be considered on its own merits, taking into account all the factors prevailing at the time and also the possible future trends. When faced with a problem of non-availability of physical resources the questions which must be posed are:

1. Is a short- or long-term maintenance required?
2. Can a suitable alternative be found?
3. Would the complete renewal of all the material or component be justifiable?
4. Is the ordering of purpose-made materials or components justifiable?
5. Is the building as a whole worthy of high capital outlay?

6. What is the estimated remaining effective life of the building in terms of the maintenance problem under consideration?

The answers to the above questions should be sufficient to enable a decision to be made.

If the physical resources are available to enable the desired maintenance work to be carried out the above questions should still be asked. For example, a major overhaul of a central heating system may, in the long term, be better if a complete new system was designed and installed together with thermal insulation measures to counteract excessive heat loss. Another problem is of course the time element; can the available resources be delivered within an acceptable time limit? If not, are other sources available? Or would it be prudent to consider the six questions posed above?

Urgency

When faced with the decision to carry out maintenance works the matter of urgency may outweigh the factors outlined above. An urgent maintenance task may be required for a number of reasons such as the repair of services which, unless rectified immediately, would render them unserviceable, which may be inconvenient, dangerous or even illegal; the repair to some part of the fabric which no longer forms a suitable barrier to the elements; the repair of a finishing which has become loose and may constitute a hazard to the normal personnel circulation within the building; and the repair of a fitting or component which is faulty and lessens the security of the premises.

When such a fault arises the paramount question which must be posed is: how urgent is urgent? Urgent is a relative term and therefore it must be established whether the repair needs to be carried out immediately, within hours or within days. If maintenance is needed immediately the costs generally will become of secondary importance and if the resources for a permanent repair are not immediately available a temporary solution will have to be found, which in turn will increase the costs since the temporary maintenance will not eliminate the need for a permanent repair or replacement. Maintenance which does not have to be carried out immediately will give time to enable the mode of maintenance necessary to be planned and controlled in such a manner so as to minimize the cost, reduce any inconvenience the work may cause and also to compare alternatives to try to achieve the best possible method in the long term. Obviously the longer the time available the greater are the chances of achieving the most economical repair.

When urgent maintenance becomes necessary the primary objective must be to have the work carried out satisfactorily in the shortest possible time. The secondary objective should be to find out how and why it became necessary. Maintenance of this nature often occurs without warning and without there being any negligence or laxity on anybody's behalf; but many items of urgent maintenance are avoidable. If routine inspections, testing, examinations and maintenance have not been carried out as planned, ordered or recommended then consideration must be given to the instigation of a more foolproof system than that which prevails at present to ensure that whenever possible urgent maintenance is avoided or reduced to a minimum.

Future use

The question of short- or long-term maintenance has already been considered in the context of the availability of physical resources and urgency and this question should also be asked when considering future use. If, for example, a certain component or fitting needs maintaining it may well be that it has already been scheduled for replacement in a different format at some future date such as the replacement of a bath by a shower unit. The question at this point in time is do we carry out the necessary maintenance on the bath? Or taking into account its future use, replace it with a shower unit by bringing forward its planned replacement date? Or alternatively do we maintain or if necessary replace the bath and delay the change of use until the bath has been used for an economic period?

The future use of the building as a whole must also be considered when deciding when and how much maintenance to carry out at any given period of time. If, for example, the lease has only a short period left and it is known that there will be a change of use or that a complete refurbishment programme has been planned for the building, the question of maintenance in all its aspects must be considered. Certain maintenance items must be carried out to fulfil legal requirements. Are these items to be carried out to the minimum or cheapest standard? Or should some effort be made to carry out the maintenance in the context of the proposed future use? Other items of maintenance in this context of future use would probably be considered under the question of urgency, as described above. If the maintenance is carried out to the minimum specification, will this have repercussions in terms of social considerations?

A number of questions have been posed above but answers cannot be given unless actual cases are studied; but the types of consideration which must be taken into account when deciding to carry out maintenance in the context of future use should now be evident.

Social considerations

Builders engaged on maintenance works, like those engaged in constructing new buildings, have an impact on society in that the results of their endeavours are left behind as an asset to the owner which may or may not improve the local environment. The principal objective should of course be to leave the local environment in an improved state or at least in no worse a state than that which existed before the work was undertaken.

The very nature of the work carried out by builders engaged in maintenance activities can create disturbances such as noise, dust, smells and the temporary interruption of services. It must, therefore, be one of the builder's objectives to recognize this social responsibility and plan the works so that any disturbance will be reduced to a minimum, particularly when working within a building where the occupants are trying to carry out their normal duties.

The owner of a building, when trying to make a decision to carry out maintenance works, must take the above social responsibilities into consideration by assessing the possible disturbances which could occur and what effect such disturbances may have on the occupants. It may be possible to plan the timing of certain maintenance activities so that they can be carried out whilst the building is unoccupied, such as during the night, at weekends or during a holiday closure. The general public may also have to be considered in this context; works to external façades of a building will have to be planned not only to reduce noise and dust levels to an acceptable amount but also from the aspects of safety to both the operatives and the general public. If the building is used during the normal course of business by the public, further consideration may have to be given as to the timing and protection aspects, since it is easier to reorganize and control employees to minimize the disturbance than it is to organize and control the general public.

The way in which maintenance works are planned, controlled and carried out, whether large or small, can increase or decrease the owner's or company's image not only through the eyes of their own staff but also those of the general public. Well-maintained buildings will create the right atmosphere conducive to personal contentment and in the case of employees this will increase morale and productivity. Good maintenance may also encourage would-be clients or customers to enter the premises, and since first impressions are very important it is prudent to project the correct image of the company by having a clean and well-maintained building in which to transact their business.

The social consequences of individuals and companies who keep their properties well maintained can be far reaching. By setting an example and establishing standards to their neighbours it can have a snowball effect, resulting in a better general environment in which to live, work or pass through. This can be readily seen by observing various areas throughout the country; shabby and poorly maintained properties are seldom isolated, they occur in groups or areas usually with a high percentage of vandalism; conversely, well-maintained properties also occur in groups or areas with low vandalism, due mainly to the example and standards set which will instil into the users a sense of pride and social responsibility. For summary chart see Fig. 1.5.

Factors influencing the decisions to adapt buildings

Adaptation of buildings has already been defined and covers a wide field of building activities, but before the work can be instigated a decision must be made to proceed with the proposed works and the factors which may influence such a decision can be listed as follows:

1. Costs.
2. Investment options.
3. Future use and life.

16

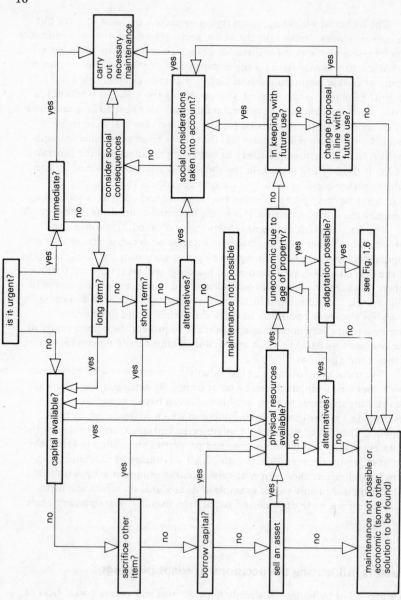

Fig. 1.5. Factors influencing the decision to carry out maintenance

4. Aesthetics.
5. Social considerations.
6. Availability of physical resources.
7. Time factors.
8. Statutory approvals.

It will be seen from the above list that there is a general similarity between the influencing factors on decisions to carry out maintenance and the influencing factors on decisions to adapt buildings. This is indeed true, but there are some special considerations to take into account when deciding to adapt buildings which are worthy of being noted.

Costs

The costs of adapting a building, like those considered for maintenance, will include labour and material. It may also be necessary to employ an architect to prepare the scheme and generally supervise the whole contract, including engaging specialist designers. If this is the case their fees will have to be added to the labour and materials costs. The capital allocation for the proposed adaptation should have been included in the annual budget, therefore the question of sacrificing some other form of expenditure should not arise, but the question of other forms of investment should not be ignored.

If the proposed adaptation is because of urgent necessity such as extra space for an expanding business or family the other investment options are often ignored by many since they do not wish to change, for personal or commercial reasons, to a larger property which may in fact be a better investment and entail overall lower costs than adapting the existing premises. Some adaptations to domestic properties are undertaken not for extra space, investment or economic considerations, but simply to impress the neighbours. Commercial and similar enterprises, however, must take into account all cost aspects if the proposed adaptation is going to be economic and they can only do this by comparing capital and running costs with other investment options.

Investment options

The common method of assessing the viability of investment options is to compare the capital outlay with the estimated future yearly returns with other forms of investment over the same period with the same amount of capital outlay. This is usually carried out by the discounted cash flow method, which is sometimes referred to as the internal rate of return. This method will be described in detail in the chapter on economics, but the basic principle should, however, be considered at this stage.

If a sum of £10 000 is invested for ten years at a compound interest rate of 8 per cent it will be worth £21 589.25 at the end of the investment period as can be seen from the following calculation:

$$A = P (1 + \frac{r}{100})^n$$

where A = amount

P = principal

r = rate of interest

n = number of years

$$A = 10\ 000 \left(1 + \frac{8}{100}\right)^{10}$$

$$= 10\ 000 \left(1 + 0.08\right)^{10}$$

$$= 10\ 000 \left(1.08\right)^{10}$$

$$= £21\ 589.25$$

If however the capital of £10 000 was invested in the adaptation of a building bringing in an anticipated net income of £1 300 for the first year, £1400 for the second year and increasing by £100 per year to realize a net income of £2200 in the tenth year, then calculating by the discounted cash flow method the internal rate of return can be shown to be 10.58 per cent, and therefore in direct comparison to investment of 8 per cent at compound interest this would be a viable project.

Discounting is a method of calculating the present value of a sum of money due in the future and is basically the reciprocal of compounding giving the basic expression of:

$$A = \frac{P}{\left(1 + \frac{r}{100}\right)^n}$$

If, for example, £100 is invested at 5 per cent for one year, it would yield £105; conversely if I wish to receive £100 in one year's time I would have to invest £95.24 at 5 per cent interest or the present-day value of £100 to be received in one year is £95.24.

Proof:

$$A = P\left(1 + \frac{r}{100}\right)^n \qquad\qquad A = \frac{P}{\left(1 + \frac{r}{100}\right)^n}$$

$$= 100\left(1 + \frac{5}{100}\right)^1 \qquad\qquad = \frac{100}{\left(1 + 0.05\right)^1}$$

$$= 100 \times 1.05 \qquad\qquad = \frac{100}{1.05}$$

$$= £105 \qquad\qquad = £95.238$$

Estimates of net future income can obviously turn out to be wrong, so therefore sensitivity calculations should be made. In the hypothetical case quoted above, if the actual net income was under- or over-estimated the revised internal rates of return would be:

Percentage of estimate	Internal rate of return (%)
70	3.54
80	6.04

90	8.37
100	10.58
110	12.67
120	14.67
130	16.61

The above results indicate that providing the actual net return is not less than 90 per cent of the estimated net return the project would still be viable when compared with the straight investment at a compound interest rate of 8 per cent. Students should not be concerned at this stage how the above figures have been calculated but they should appreciate that such calculations are necessary if a decision to adapt buildings is to be made.

Cost-in-use is another way of studying alternatives. This method considers the total cost of the proposed adaptation over its whole life and can be expressed as:

Total cost = Capital cost + operation costs + maintenance costs.

The operation cost would include such outgoings as heating, lighting, power, labour charges for services and insurances. These costs will occur at different points in time, they should therefore be discounted to a common time base which is usually their present-day value. If the hypothetical case under consideration was subjected to a cost-in-use study the total cost would be £16 120.74 if the following costs were taken into account:

Capital cost	£10 000
Operation costs	£700 per annum
Maintenance costs	£200 per annum
Renewal cost of a major item	£120 due in 5 years
Life	10 years
Discount rate	8 per cent.

The total net income is £17 500; therefore on the result of the above cost-in-use study the project is viable.

Two points should be made at this stage – first, inflation and capital borrowing interest rates have not been taken into account since they would be a common factor in all the comparisons, and second, taxation and investment allowances have not been considered since at this stage the study is concerned primarily with principles and not with the finer points of accountancy. It should also be noted that the general use of discounted cash flow and cost-in-use techniques is for the comparison of various building design concepts rather than an exercise in initial decision making to adapt buildings. It can therefore be concluded that all sources of investment should be considered not simply whether to invest a capital sum to secure a return as interest, but also the various types and details of a number of designs to see which would yield the best return on the investment over the anticipated life of the proposed project.

Future use and life

The question of the future use of a building when deciding to carry out a programme of adaptation must be fully considered. The questions to be asked are similar to those already noted when considering the decision to carry out maintenance work and are mainly concerned in deciding whether the proposed adaptation should be planned as a short- or long-term project in the context of the building's future use.

The future life of the building will mean that other considerations must be taken into account. The initial question of short- or long-term design is self evident. We can design so that the life of the proposed adaptation will terminate at approximately the same time as the existing building, or the design can be based on normal practices which will usually give the proposed adaptation a longer anticipated life than the existing structure. A third consideration is also possible; if it has been decided to carry out the proposed adaptation by normal design practices it may be worth while to refurbish the existing building so that its anticipated life is extended to that of the proposed adaptation.

If the third option is to be considered it must be appreciated that this cannot be done in the context of future life alone; costs, investment options, social considerations and statutory approvals must also be taken into account. Decisions of this nature are not easy to make and it cannot be overstressed that all aspects must be fully analysed very carefully if the correct decision is going to be made.

Aesthetics

The term 'aesthetics' comes from the Greek word 'aisthanesthai', meaning to perceive, and is the laws and principles determining beauty, art and taste, all of which are subjective. It is therefore very difficult to state what is or is not aesthetically acceptable in any particular situation. If an adaptation project has been conceived on the basic principles of function its appearance may be of secondary importance to the owner, but the external or internal appearance can have other effects. A perfectly functional adaptation or extension can be designed and constructed but its outward appearance can also be completely out of balance with the existing or surrounding buildings which may make it unacceptable to the neighbouring owners or planning authority.

Architects are trained to consider aesthetics as part of the whole design process and therefore if a competent architect is appointed to specify, design and supervise the proposed adaptation the problem of the external or internal appearance being out of character or balance with its surroundings should be lessened. Unfortunately there is no legal obligation to employ a trained and qualified architect to carry out this type of work. A walk around any built-up area in this country will show quite clearly, judging by the many ponderous appendages, that many owners are only concerned with functional aspects, and providing these adaptations meet all the legal requirements some local authorities are prepared to pass their designs.

It must be stressed, however, that functional and aesthetic considerations must not be treated in isolation; the two must be blended to produce an adaptation which will give the client value for money throughout the anticipated life of the building and at the same time fulfil the function for which it was designed.

Social considerations

The comments which have already been made regarding the social considerations when deciding to carry out maintenance work are equally valid when considering the possibility of carrying out adaptation activities, except that often by the very nature of the proposed work the problems can be greater. Adaptation activities can often cause more disturbance than general maintenance work and therefore these activities will require a higher degree of planning and control to reduce such disturbances to an acceptable level.

The aftermath of the work should also be considered before any decision is taken to carry out the adaptation of a building. Will the proposed changes be acceptable to the people who will have to work or use the modification or extension? Should these people be consulted about the proposal and its basic design concepts so that a general understanding of all their views can be established before the final decisions are taken? Will the work be acceptable to people not directly involved with its use or will the proposed adaptation cause resentment on the grounds of appearance or the belief that such works are unnecessary or undesirable? It must be remembered that although not strictly measurable, goodwill or good relationships can go a long way in helping to operate a successful business or making life pleasant.

The disturbance which may be caused to the occupants or users of a building which is being considered for adaptation will have to be taken into account. The nature of the works will determine whether normal usage of the premises is possible during the construction period or whether it will be necessary to make some alternative arrangements or find some extra or temporary accommodation for the users. The effect of such arrangements on the morale of those involved and any likely effects on trading will also have to be considered before the final decisions to proceed can be made.

Availability of physical resources

The adaptation of a building will usually involve predominantly the use of new materials and components throughout the entire works, therefore the matching of materials in some areas with the surrounding material (as discussed previously in the context of roof tiles) when considering maintenance decisions should not normally arise. Blend with adjacent existing materials, however, may well be important. If the physical resources are not available to achieve an exact blend it may be possible to use an entirely different material to obtain an acceptable and tasteful contrast.

When specifying materials and components for the proposed work the availability of all physical resources should be taken into account, but by the time it comes to actually ordering the resources the supply situation may have changed. If this is the case alternative or acceptable substitute materials or components will have to be found unless the project is to be delayed until the first choice of physical resources are available. The question of comparable costs and life expectancy in comparison with the original specification will have to be considered to see if such a change is viable or acceptable to all parties.

Unfortunately changes of this nature are not necessarily as simple as they may appear to be at the first consideration. A change in specification may have to meet the planning and/or building control officer's approval before it can be implemented and this may not be forthcoming. There may be a time delay whilst agreement is reached. This may in turn lead to a change in the estimated contract sum which could make the whole proposal uneconomic.

It can be seen from the brief comments above that the availability of physical resources is an important aspect when making a decision to carry out the adaptation of a building and that these aspects should be borne in mind from the initial briefing stage right through all the design steps up to the actual construction period.

Time factors

'Time is money' is a well-known cliché but in the context of decision making it is very true. Time is expended in briefing the architect; coming to an agreement on the overall format, preparing the necessary specification, drawings and where applicable the Bill of Quantities; obtaining any necessary planning permission and Building Regulation approval; negotiating for and evaluating tender documents and the actual contract period. Capital will have to be raised to finance the project and the longer the loan period the greater will be the interest charges incurred. Therefore it is in the interest of all the parties involved to keep each phase and consequently the overall period as short as practicable. Planning permission for the proposed adaptation will also have a time limit of between three and five years depending on the type of planning permission given; therefore the proposed project should be commenced within this period otherwise the whole exercise may have to be repeated.

Apart from the length of time taken from instigation to occupation the time at which the works are to be carried out is also important. Adaptation activities generally lead to some degree of upheaval and disturbance and therefore the contract period should be planned in the light of the nature of the proposed works and the type of occupancy which is using the building to be adapted. In the case of short duration works, the annual closure for holidays would be the ideal time for major work to take place. Where there is no holiday closure period or the works are of a longer period of time, alternative or temporary arrangements would have to be made to enable the normal business to be carried out. Time must be allowed to acquaint regular or would-be clients or customers with the temporary arrangements so that the enterprise will not suffer.

In domestic situations the most advantageous time to carry out the proposed work would be from April until September, thus avoiding the worst of the winter and enabling the work to proceed with the minimum amount of interruption due to inclement weather. Where the domestic premises have to be vacated to enable the work to proceed the reverse may well be true since temporary accommodation may be easier to find in the October to March period, and indeed could also be cheaper.

The above consideration of overall time factors and contract periods may have some influence in the way in which the works are planned and carried out by indicating the best operations sequence, to cause the least disturbance over the minimum time period, or by indicating the necessary labour force and plant requirements to ensure that the contract is completed within the shortest practicable time limit.

Statutory approvals

Before any adaptation work can commence certain statutory approvals may be required under current legislation such as the Town and Country Planning Act 1971 (as amended by the 1972 Act); the Local Government Act 1972; the Public Health Act 1936; the Clean Air Act 1956. the Public Health Act 1961; the Fire Precautions Act 1971 and the Health and Safety at Work etc. Act 1974. Some of these Acts and their relevance to the maintenance and adaptation of buildings will be dealt with in greater detail in Chapter 4 on legislation but basically the statutory approvals which may be required are planning permission and Building Regulation approval.

In the context of the adaptation of buildings, the need to obtain planning permission may not be necessary since the proposed work could fall into the category of 'permitted development' as laid down in the Town and Country Planning General Development Order 1963 as amended. If the proposed adaptation is not a development then again planning permission is not required. What in fact constitutes a development is an involved topic but if any doubt exists an application can be made to the local planning authority to determine whether planning permission is required under Section 53 of the Town and Country Planning Act 1971. If planning permission is required an application can be made for:

1. *Outline planning permission:* this is basically an application for approval in principle of the proposed development before any actual details have been prepared. If the application is refused a lot of time, effort and money would be saved by not applying for full planning permission in the first instance. If the outline planning permission is granted it will be necessary to submit, at a later stage, the necessary details for approval of reserved matters.

2. *Approval of reserved matters:* these are matters reserved at the stage when outline planning permission is given to be considered at a later date when details are available. An application for approval must be made within the period stipulated in the permission or if not stipulated as laid down in Section 42 of the 1971 Act.

3. *Full planning permission:* this is a detailed application where the full details of the proposed adaptation are known and submitted.

If the time limit of any planning permission is going to expire before work commences, an application for renewal of time-limited permission under Section 41 or 42 of the 1971 Act can be made to the planning authority. If an application for planning permission accompanied by the

necessary certificates and notices is submitted and is granted, Building
Regulation approval may still be required.

Building Regulation approval is required in the majority of cases, the
exemptions being specified in Section 71 of the Public Health Act 1936 and
set out in Regulation A5 of the Building Regulations 1976. Like planning
permission, the approval given under the Building Regulations has a time
limit during which the works must be commenced or re-approval will have
to be sought; in this case the time limit is three years.

It may also be necessary to obtain the approval of the appointed local
fire officer to ensure that the proposals are adequate in terms of means of
escape in case of fire either under Part E of the Building Regulations or the
Fire Precautions Act 1971. Many county authorities also require that
adequate means of access for the fire brigade are also included in the proposal
before permission to proceed can be granted.

Obtaining all the necessary statutory approvals before a proposed
adaptation to a building can proceed can be a complex procedure, and if
not presented in the correct format can lead to lengthy delays before
permission is finally obtained; therefore if the proposed adaptation comes
under the category which requires planning permission it is important that
the person in charge of the design is qualified and experienced in negotiating
with the various authorities if a successful conclusion is to be achieved within
a reasonable time period. For summary chart see Fig. 1.6.

Terotechnology

Whilst considering the basic principles of the maintenance and adaptation of
buildings, students should be aware of the concept of terotechnology, which
can be defined as 'a combination of management, financial, engineering and
other practices applied to physical assets in pursuit of economic life-cycle
costs'. The term terotechnology is derived from the Greek word 'tereo',
meaning 'I care', and requires no new techniques or disciplines and indeed
has been practised by many people purely by a commonsense approach to the
care of their physical assets throughout their life cycle. Terotechnology techniques can be applied throughout all industries, but our particular study is
confined to the building industry.

The basic idea of terotechnology is to bring together all the different
disciplines to make their contribution to optimizing life-cycle costs which
include all the costs in acquiring, using and caring for the physical assets of
the enterprise. The designer when formulating his plans should be concerned
not only with their primary functions and appearance but also with the
building's reliability and maintainability. This design function extends not
only to the structure itself but also to all the finishes, fittings, services and
components within the building. To enable the designer to implement this
aspect of design he needs to rely on feedback information giving data on the
past performance of all aspects of buildings in use to enable him to improve
on past performance and therefore achieve a balance between the client's
initial requirements and optimum life-cycle costs.

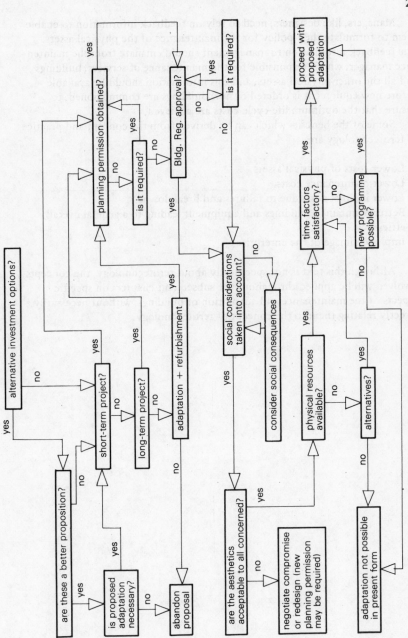

Fig. 1.6. Factors influencing decisions to adapt buildings

Managers, like designers, need to rely on feedback information to enable them to formulate their policy for the maintenance of the physical assets. The feedback information to management should emanate from the maintenance manager, who is responsible for the maintenance of services, buildings and all the other physical assets, and this information should be available before new equipment is ordered or new buildings are commissioned, to ensure that the optimum life-cycle costs are achieved.

Some of the benefits which can be derived from the concept and practice of terotechnology are:

1. Lower costs of physical assets.
2. Lower maintenance costs.
3. Lower indirect costs due to failures and breakdowns.
4. Better maintained buildings and equipment leading to a general overall efficiency.
5. Improved image of the enterprise.

Although this text is not specifically about terotechnology, the concepts involved will be applied throughout the subsequent chapters on specific aspects of the maintenance and adaptation of buildings, without necessarily directly relating them to the concept of terotechnology.

Chapter 2

Design considerations

The objective of this chapter is to show the way by which designers, their designs and design procedures can lead to a reduction in maintenance work and improvements in the quality and efficiency of maintenance works. To achieve this objective the basic design procedures must be understood and a realization that unless the designer is given a reasonable amount of flexibility in both design detail and cost implications, the best that he can hope to achieve is a poor compromise which may give the client a building at a relatively low capital cost, but in terms of cost-in-use the total expenditure over the anticipated life of the building could be uneconomic.

As stated in the previous chapter, it is not a legal requirement to engage an architect to undertake building design work; indeed, an architect may have to employ specialist designers to assist him or carry out particular aspects of the design work. I have therefore chosen to use the all-embracing term of designer for the leader of the entire design team, although in the majority of cases this may well be a qualified architect. To fully appreciate the designer's problems it is first necessary to understand the sequence of stages through which the design passes and the other parties which can become involved.

The first stage in any design concept does not usually involve the designer but merely the building owner, which may be an individual or a very complex organization. The decision must first be made by the building owner that he wants to invest in a new structure and he must have some idea as to the basic requirements. In well organized and experienced companies the initial brief prepared for the designer can be very detailed, whereas from the inexperienced individual the initial brief may consist of 'I want a three-bedroom house on this plot of land for not more than £x.' Having decided to proceed with the proposal the building owner must now select a designer; this may be done by past experience, recommendation, or by enquiring of a number of designers to see if they are experienced in this form of construction and if their work load is such that they can accept another brief.

The major services offered by an architect or designer are:

1. The complete design and detail of the proposed building to the client's satisfaction in terms of cost, reliability, maintainability and a building which is aesthetically acceptable.
2. The administration of the whole project from its initial briefing stage to final completion including meeting all the necessary permissions and approvals, advising on the selection of a suitable contractor and overseeing during the actual contract period.

It cannot be overstressed that if a successful conclusion is to be achieved there must be a good rapport between the client and designer based on mutual understanding, trust and respect.

The brief

Few clients have any real knowledge of the information a designer needs at the initial brief stage, the exceptions being clients who have been through the process before or clients requiring buildings of a special nature such as hospitals, schools and certain manufacturing complexes. These latter clients usually receive specialist advice in preparing their initial brief for the chosen designer; the specialist advisers are very often within their own employ. The detailed brief which arises out of the client's initial brief is normally the result of a number of meetings and discussions between the two parties. The designer will formulate the detailed brief for the client's approval before the real detailed design begins; this is to prevent a great deal of abortive work being carried out.

Basically the information required from the client by the designer to enable the discussions to take place and the detailed brief formulated are:

1. The basic usage of the proposed building and any multiple uses such as part offices, part showroom and part manufacturing areas.
2. The basic areas required for the usages given above.
3. Population densities and male-to-female ratios for the different areas.
4. Any specific requirements as to types and nature of machinery, preparation areas, assembly areas, computer rooms or any other form of accommodation.
5. Any specific instructions as to basic decor requirements.
6. Any specific requirements as to services and service facilities.
7. Some indication as to the time scale envisaged for the whole project.
8. Any general or specific maintenance requirements which need to be considered at the design stage.

9.   Capital available to finance the proposal.

Sometimes the question of cost is not considered at this initial briefing stage but is delayed until the designer has had time to explore some initial ideas and solutions so that he is in a better position to advise his client on cost aspects.

The designer will make his decisions as to the assistance he requires from specialist designers or engineers and quantity surveyors; from meetings and discussions with them should emerge the sketch proposals together with an estimation of the capital, maintenance and operational costs of the proposed building. General arrangement drawings should be submitted showing the basic layout in the form of small-scale plans, elevations and possibly a perspective drawing, together with a report as to the general specification, structural loadings, services to be installed and maintenance considerations for submission to the client for approval. If it is a large project a small-scale model of the scheme could also be made and submitted to clarify the designer's intentions.

Preparation of contract documents

The documents which are needed to enable a contract to be drawn up for the construction of the proposed building will vary according to the value of the contract, but the basic documents are:

1.   Specification of proposed works.
2.   Working drawings.
3.   Schedules.
4.   Bill of quantities.

In the case of low price contracts the bill of quantities may not be prepared; instead the invited contractors will tender on the basis of the specification and drawings, which will mean that the contractor will have to prepare his own 'bill of quantities' to enable his estimator to formulate a tender figure.

The specification

This is a document which, although its preparation is the responsibility of the designer, can be written by him or the quantity surveyor. It has two main functions:

1.   Together with the drawings, it is the brief from which the quantity surveyor will prepare the bill of quantities.
2.   Together with the drawings and the bill of quantities, it can be used by the contractor's estimator to enable him to prepare his unit rates and so obtain a tender figure.

There is no standard format for the presentation of a specification for building works but the two common methods in use are:

1. Based on the sequence of trade sections as set out in the Standard Method of Measurement of Building Works which is jointly sponsored by the Royal Institution of Chartered Surveyors and The National Federation of Building Trades Employers.
2. Based on defined areas of the building such as basement and ground floor. The specification would set out all the work required in each area and could be sub-divided into sections covering general aspects, materials and workmanship, or alternatively these can be specified together under each area section.

Working drawings

A set of working drawings are produced primarily to communicate to the builder the designer's intentions, and to achieve this objective they should contain sufficient information to enable the builder to carry out his part of the contract accurately and efficiently. The drawings must therefore be accurate, easily read, contain sufficient detail, data and information to enable the construction work to proceed without constant reference to the designer for more information. They should be able to be read in conjunction with the specification and not prepared in such a manner that they are duplicating the information contained in the specification, since this may lead to drawings which are overcrowded with information, making them difficult to read and assimilate.

The Building Research Establishment carried out a programme of research into working drawings in use and published in 1973 a current paper (CP 18/73) which stresses the uncertainty on site which can be caused if the information sent to site is inadequate, since either the work cannot be carried out or there is a danger of mistakes being made. Obviously if the latter are not noticed during the construction period this could lead to maintenance problems in the future. The main causes of uncertainties on site leading to queries found by the research programme are:

1. Unco-ordinated drawings – conflicting information from separate sources.
2. Errors – items of information incorrect.
3. Failures in transmission – information not sent to site but available elsewhere.
4. Inadequate detail – parts of design insufficiently explained.
5. Omissions – items of information accidently missing.
6. Poor presentation – information complete but difficult to read.

The builder has three main areas of operation for which he needs comprehensive data from the designer in the form of a specification, working drawings, schedules and a bill of quantities and these are:

1. *Ordering of all forms of materials:* this requires a specification and working drawings, both of which should be related to the bill of quantities. He will also need data and details of any special works or components on a supply only or a supply and fix basis.

2. *Organizing labour and plant resources:* this requires a specification setting out the quality of workmanship required and the nature of any particular method which must be employed together with the necessary working drawings.

3. *Planning and programming the contract:* this will require full working drawings giving complete information on all aspects of the project together with any site operations, access or noise level restraints being imposed and also the contractural conditions.

The manner in which the working drawings are presented to communicate some of the above stated data will often be dictated by the method of preparing the set of drawings prevailing in the office of origin. There are several conventional methods in operation but many sets are in fact a combination of these traditional methods. Sets of working drawings can be prepared in any of the following ways:

1. *Trade sequence:* each trade has a set of drawings giving all the necessary data. This method is only suitable if each trade sequence can be successfully isolated, otherwise there can be a considerable amount of duplication of details due to the overlapping of trades and this duplication can lead to errors and ambiguities, giving rise to mistakes, which in turn can result in unnecessary and avoidable maintenance in the future. Due to the complex nature of buildings today this system is not very often employed.

2. *Operational sequence:* in this method drawings are prepared for each operation and are usually supplemented by an operational bill of quantities. The difficulty with this method is that at the time of preparation the builder's operational sequence can only be assumed unless the builder happens to form part of the design team. It may a good method from the designer's viewpoint but it is not always practicable from the builder's standing, since his actual operational sequence may not follow that of the designer's. If this is the case he will have to refer to several drawings to abstract information, and similarly, when ordering materials, particularly in terms of bulk orders, several documents may have to be consulted to obtain all the necessary data and this continual cross referencing may lead to omissions and errors.

3. *Information required:* this is probably the best method of presentation for a set of working drawings since it will follow the standard managerial questions of what? where? and how? These questions can be answered by component, assembly and location drawings respectively showing what the component is, how it is to be made and assembled, and where it is relative to the building as a whole.

The current edition of the Standard Method of Measurement of Building Works (SMM6) under clause A5 sets out the types of drawings required to fully implement the document and they are as follows:

1. *Block plan:* to identify site and outline of buildings in relation to Town Planning or other wider context.

2. *Site plan:* location of site showing means of access and general layout.

3. *General location drawing:* showing the position occupied by the various spaces in a building, general construction and the location of principal elements.

4. *Component details:* to give all necessary data for the manufacture and assembly of components.

5. *Bill diagrams:* drawn information to be provided as part of the bill of quantities as an alternative to lengthy descriptions.

Whatever mode of presentation is chosen it cannot be over emphasized that incomplete, inaccurate and/or ambiguous drawings and details together with the reader's misinterpretation may lead to unnecessary or avoidable maintenance in the future. Research has shown that 54 per cent of mistakes in construction can be attributed to the design stage, whereas only 24 per cent and 22 per cent are attributed to the construction stage and other stages respectively.

Schedules

In most sets of working drawings, especially on large projects, there is always information which is repetitive and this type of data can be presented in the form of a schedule which can be read in conjunction with the working drawings. The form which schedules can take are:

1. *List schedules:* these, as their name implies, are merely a list of similar items with an identification as to where they occur in the building. Suitable items which can be listed in this manner are ironmongery, internal finishes and decorations.
2. *Tabulated schedules:* these are the most popular form, consisting of column headings matched to a vertical location or identification column on the right-hand side. Doors, windows, drainage and sanitary fitments are suitable for scheduling in this manner.
3. *Drawings with schedules:* these are useful where a simple detail or outline can be used as a positive identification to the item or items being scheduled. Typical examples are doors, windows, joinery fittings, precast concrete components and reinforcement schedules prepared by the structural engineer.

Schedules are used by the quantity surveyor to enable him to prepare the bill of quantities accurately and easily without the need for constant reference to the working drawings. The builder can use schedules to assist him in the preparation of his estimate and on site they are useful since all similar information has been collated into one source, thus giving an overall quick reference to that particular aspect.

The preparation of schedules, like that of the specification and working drawings, must be meticulous, since when dealing with repetitive items mistakes and omissions can easily occur which can lead to misinterpretation and constructional faults. These may not become apparent for some time after the completion of the works, giving rise to unnecessary or avoidable maintenance.

Bill of quantities

The bill of quantities is a document which has the primary function of assisting the builder in estimating the cost of a project. It is usually prepared by a qualified quantity surveyor in the sequence and manner set out in The Standard Method of Measurement for Building Works, the exception being when the anticipated value of the project is such that a bill of quantities is not considered justifiable. In these cases the builder would abstract his own quantities of materials and labour from the specification and drawings supplied by the designer.

The quantity surveyor will prepare the bill of quantities using the working drawings, schedules and specification supplied by the designer, and inevitably, if there are mistakes in these documents, they will appear in the bill of quantities unless the quantity surveyor discovers them and in collaboration with the designer has the details, schedules or specification amended. The quantity surveyor is trying to convey to the builder the quality, quantity and nature of the materials, works and labour needed to carry out the proposed project to a satisfactory conclusion so that a real estimate of cost can be obtained. The building owner at this stage does not know what the project will cost in terms of capital costs; he has obviously been advised of possible costs by the designer and quantity surveyor whose opinions would have been based on similar projects and current price trends.

Although the construction errors leading to unnecessary or avoidable future maintenance emanating from a bill of quantities are usually low, confusion can be caused where there is conflict between the bill of quantities, schedules, working drawings and specification leading to a mistrust of all four types of document by the builder. Any project which does not have a harmonious team with mutual respect for one another can result in a building of low quality and hence low performance with high maintenance during its anticipated life. For a summary of the basic design steps see Fig. 2.1.

Implications of adaptation

Before considering the implications of the adaptation of buildings it is a useful exercise to consider why buildings become empty and available, and also why adaptation may be a better answer than demolition and rebuilding. There are many contributory factors, such as changes in technology, changes in patterns of transportation, decentralization policies and changes in social needs.

34

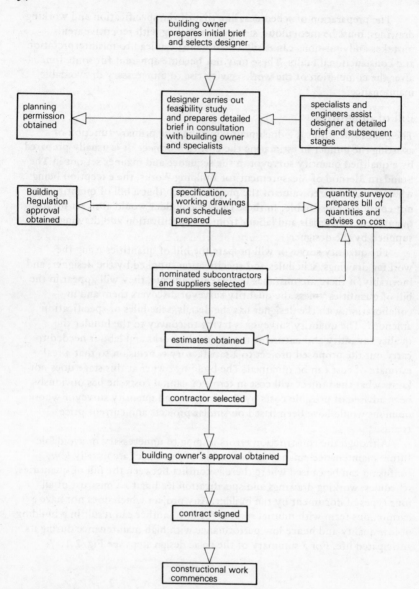

Fig. 2.1. Summary of basic design steps

The boxes in the figure contain the following text:

- building owner prepares initial brief and selects designer
- designer carries out feasibility study and prepares detailed brief in consultation with building owner and specialists
- planning permission obtained
- specialists and engineers assist designer at detailed brief and subsequent stages
- Building Regulation approval obtained
- specification, working drawings and schedules prepared
- quantity surveyor prepares bill of quantities and advises on cost
- nominated subcontractors and suppliers selected
- estimates obtained
- contractor selected
- building owner's approval obtained
- contract signed
- constructional work commences

New technologies and methods of manufacture often dictate a different form of building to house the new processes and industries. These changes had a peak during the early 1960s when the Government of the day was encouraging manufacturing firms to move out of the cities to the new towns and also to areas of high unemployment. The change from predominantly rail transportation of goods to road transportation using the new motorways also encouraged firms to move to areas easily served by the new road network rather than remain in the congested urban areas. Government aid in the form of investment grants also added impetus to this movement.

Decentralization left in its wake a considerable stock of industrial buildings which were too large for small businesses to take over in their existing form. The new development areas not only gave the firms which moved better communications, but also room for future expansion not possible in their city locations. When these firms moved some of their workforce moved with them, leaving behind housing accommodation, generally of the older types of property, and this in turn reflected in a number of other businesses and social concerns closing due to lack of support. The empty buildings that were left behind often soon became derelict and vandalized because no maintenance or security was being carried out to keep them in good order, since no suitable tenants could be found. In many cases it was the ideal opportunity to demolish the old out-of-date building stock and redevelop. Gradually it became evident that many of these buildings could be successfully adapted to suit small firms, large dwellings could be adapted, modernized and converted into a number of smaller units of accommodation.

At first the finance institutions were reluctant to advance the capital for the adaptation and rehabilitation of these buildings on the grounds of high risk and possible low profitability, but the finance is now becoming available since it has been shown that in many cases the proper adaptation of these types of buildings can be of low risk and profitable. This new movement towards the adaptation of suitable units of old building stock is reviving some of the inner city areas by attracting small firms and private residents, both of which are essential to achieve a balanced economy.

When buildings which are too large for a small firm or family in their present state become vacant, it cannot be automatically assumed that they can be adapted easily and successfully for multi-occupations or multi-occupants. A very careful and detailed feasibility study should be carried out to establish:

1. Existing usage classification.
2. Condition of structure and fabric.
3. Possibilities in terms of change of use.
4. Problems associated with 3 above.
5. Commercial viability of any such adaptation.

Since this text is concerned not with design detail but with the implications of adaptation, some simple examples should be sufficient to clarify the above considerations – see Figs. 2.2 to 2.4.

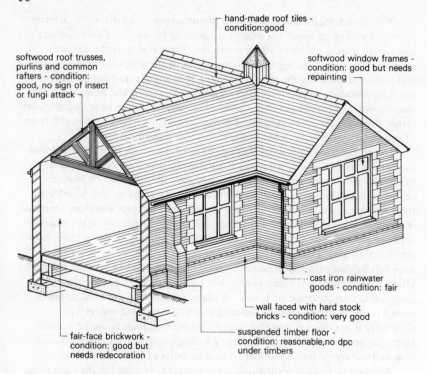

hand-made roof tiles - condition:good

softwood roof trusses, purlins and common rafters - condition: good, no sign of insect or fungi attack

softwood window frames - condition: good but needs repainting

cast iron rainwater goods - condition: fair

wall faced with hard stock bricks - condition: very good

fair-face brickwork - condition: good but needs redecoration

suspended timber floor - condition: reasonable,no dpc under timbers

Building type - single storey with mainly large spaces - existing use school - age *c.*1870.

Site data - basically courtyard/island type in a semi-rural area with approximately 40% site coverage excluding small group of outbuildings in very poor condition.

Considerations - is building listed? internal daylight factor is good therefore could be used for studios or small workrooms for light assembly or similar work. Large rooms can easily be subdivided to form smaller units, ceiling can be lowered by either attached or suspended techniques.

Problems: large room volumes, poor thermal insulation, existing heating system inadequate and in poor condition, existing floor unable to accept loadings in excess of 3.0 kN/m2.

Advantages: ample space for car parking and delivery access, room for expansion at rear of site, location rural but within reach of main roads and nearest town. General fabric in good condition with anticipated future life of twenty-five years.

Fig. 2.2. Implications of adaptation — Example 1

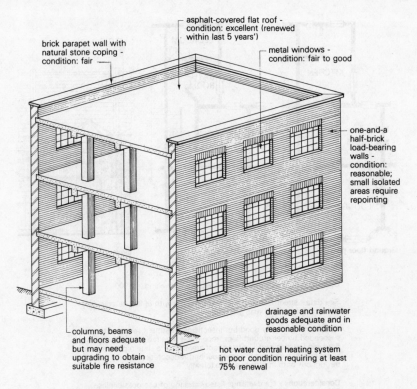

brick parapet wall with
natural stone coping -
condition: fair

asphalt-covered flat roof -
condition: excellent (renewed
within last 5 years')

metal windows -
condition: fair to good

one-and-a
half-brick
load-bearing
walls -
condition:
reasonable;
small isolated
areas require
repointing

columns, beams
and floors adequate
but may need
upgrading to obtain
suitable fire resistance

drainage and rainwater
goods adequate and in
reasonable condition

hot water central heating system
in poor condition requiring at least
75% renewal

Building type - 3-storey with large repetitive spaces - existing use
single occupancy factory - age c1880.

Site data - corner site in urban area with 60% site coverage having all
spare site space at rear with access from side road.

Considerations - is building listed? change of use possibilities - light
industrial units occupying one or more floors, craft workshops,
laboratories, museum or exhibition units.

Problems - configuration of internal columns limiting layout design,
possibility of extra means of escape provisions, upgrading building
to comply with Parts E,F,FF and G of Building Regulations, internal
services inadequate for multi-occupational use, necessitating
complete redesign and renewal.

Advantages - reasonable vehicle access to rear of building with limited
parking places, easy access to main commercial and trading areas,
good local transport facilities, labour availability should present
little or no problems. Anticipated future life thirty years.

Fig. 2.3. Implications of adaptation — Example 2

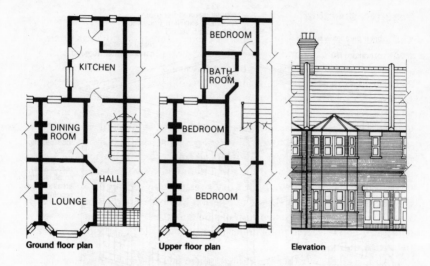

Ground floor plan **Upper floor plan** **Elevation**

Building type - 2-storey terraced Victorian dwelling *c.*1900

Site data - street frontage site in urban area with 80% site coverage with small front and rear garden areas.

Condition - generally good but insecticide treatment required to suspended timber ground floor, repointing required beneath upper floor window sills, small isolated roof areas require slate replacements, all internal services require overhaul and redecoration required throughout both internally and externally.

Considerations - are dwellings listed? change of use possibilities. Office accommodation in one or two units, bed/sitting room accommodation with shared toilet facilities or self-contained flats.

Problems - redesigning internal layout to provide acceptable accommodation and circulation, upgrading structure to comply with current Building Regulations and providing suitable means of excape in case of fire, if divided into more than one unit, provision of minimum areas suitable for type of usage, no car parking provision possible.

Advantages - well sited to local amenities, provision of small unit accommodation in high demand, anticipated future life up to fifty years depending on nature and amount of adaptation works carried out.

Fig. 2.4. Implications of adaptation – Example 3

Materials selection

The designers of the past had a limited choice of materials such as brick, stone, metal and glass and these were incorporated into their designs with confidence which was based not on the physical laws controlling the material's behaviour, but on its long history and proven performance record. Today's designer is confronted with a very wide range of materials from which he can make his selection; this is due mainly to increased technological knowledge in the manufacturing industries of man-made materials as opposed to those obtained from natural sources. These materials have the advantage of allowing a high percentage of off-site assembly and prefabrication to be carried out, reducing the need for a vast number of highly skilled craftsmen on site; also they are generally of a dry construction technique which has considerably reduced the drying out period in modern constructions. The same argument can be applied to traditional materials which can now be made into prefabricated units under factory-controlled conditions away from the actual building site.

All materials, whether traditional or new, will deteriorate with age and those in external situations are more vulnerable than those used internally. The main objectives of the designer in choosing his materials are:

1. Fulfilling the client's functional requirements.
2. Fulfilling these functional requirements over the anticipated life of the building within reasonable maintenance cost limits.
3. Keeping the costs within the client's budget for construction cost.
4. Achieving the above objectives whilst designing a building which is aesthetically acceptable to all concerned.

To obtain all four objectives is not an easy task for the designer, particularly when consideration is given for using new materials and techniques.

The designer, in his endeavour to fulfil the above objectives, will very often use new materials and techniques which although approved and tested have not withstood the test of time in the built situation. He may be unfamiliar with the limitations of the material and its interaction with other materials and components and therefore his design and specification may unwittingly be incorrect, ambiguous or inconclusive. Similarly the contractor may be unfamiliar with the material or technique and carry out the execution on site in an unsuitable manner which, as with faulty design, will lead ultimately to a breakdown of the material or a weakness emerging in the final structure leading to costly maintenance.

It follows therefore that the designer, to achieve a successful result, must have a thorough understanding of the behaviour of the materials he is specifying together with a design appreciation of the element of which they form part, the interactions and relationships of adjacent materials and components, the influence of the natural elements and the working environment within the enclosure.

Deterioration is the process of becoming worse and in the context of building materials and components it can be said to be the transition from

40

fulfilling to not fulfilling their intended function, whereas durability is the rate at which deterioration takes place. As previously stated, all building materials deteriorate over their life span due very often to weathering and fair use. A distinction must be made between visual and actual deterioration. A painted surface can be said to have deteriorated simply because it has lost its initial gloss or has become dirty but it is still adequately fulfilling its function of giving protection to the surface to which it was applied.

Many examples can be given as to the results of incorrect or inadequate material specification, faulty design and workmanship, but this would require a volume to itself. However, the consequences of deterioration and defects will be considered in greater detail in Chapter 5. The designer must therefore rely on his technical knowledge, design skills, manufacturers' data, test reports, research publications, feedback information and case studies to achieve a satisfactory selection of materials and components for his design.

Information sources

The sources of information available on materials, components and techniques to both designer and contractor are very wide ranging and vary from official documents to personal assessments contained in feedback reports. The following is a selection of some of these sources:

British Standards

These are publications issued by the British Standards Institution of which some 1500 are directly related to the construction industry and are presented in four formats:

1. *British Standards:* these give recommendations for a minimum standard of quality and testing for materials and components. Each standard is numbered and prefixed BS.

2. *Codes of Practice:* these are recommendations for good practice to be followed during design, manufacture, construction, installation and maintenance with a view to safety, quality, economy and fitness for the intended purpose. Each code is numbered and prefixed CP or BS.

3. *Draft for Development:* these are issued instead of a British Standard when there is a lack of information to make firm recommendations, particularly when dealing with new materials, components or techniques. Each draft is numbered and prefixed DD.

4. *Published Document:* these are publications which cannot be classified in any of the above given formats. Each document is numbered and prefixed PD.

It must be noted that British Standard publications are only recommendations and are therefore not legally enforceable and compliance is therefore voluntary; however, some legal documents such as the Building Regulations, refer directly to British Standards and accept them as deemed to satisfy specification. All materials and components complying with the appropriate British Standard are marked with the British Standards Institution kitemark symbol and this will give the specifier and user the assurance that the product has been made in accordance with the minimum requirements laid down in that particular British Standard.

British Standards can be purchased from the Sales Department at 101 Pentonville Road, London N1 9ND either as individual documents or in the form of a compendium known as BS Handbook No. 3 which gives summaries of over 1200 British Standards for building, and supplies the basic data of the particular standard, omitting data on test methods and production procedures; this is the main concern of the product manufacturer rather than the specifier.

Building Research Establishment

This is a group of laboratories within the Department of the Environment which carries out programmes of research and development appertaining to all aspects of the construction industry. The Building Research Establishment also provides assistance when required on the committees formulating Building Regulations and British Standards. Another function of the establishment is to answer technical queries and give advice on construction and design problems. The Building Research Establishment is divided into six departments, namely:

1. *The Materials and Structure Department:* the main aim of this department is to advance the scientific knowledge of the behaviour of materials, structures and geotechnics and apply this knowledge in an advantageous and economical manner.

2. *The Environment Department:* this department is basically concerned with design, performance and the use of buildings. The department provides the data required by designers including services, energy problems, construction plant and other engineering services.

3. *The Planning and Construction Department:* this department carries out research and studies in the use of resources in the industry such as capital, materials and labour. It is also involved with research into urban planning problems.

4. *The Fire Research Department:* this department operates under the Department of the Environment and the Fire Officers' Committee which is an association of fire insurance companies. The department researches and investigates all aspects of fire hazards, with the main objective of limiting both the material and human costs of fire damage.

5. *The Princes Risborough Laboratory:* this department concentrates its research on timber and wood-based materials to obtain data on the properties,

performance, methods of processing, methods of jointing and protecting timber of all types.

6. Communication and Services: the primary function of this department is to communicate and publish the findings of the other five departments and this is done in the form of monthly digests, current papers, building science abstracts, technical information leaflets and books. It also promotes and produces film and slide packages together with lecture notes, and operates the Building Research Advisory Service, which offers advice on any constructional problem within its own competence. If a query can be answered by existing publications the service is free but if special investigation or study is required a charge is made to cover the staff time involved. The publications of the Building Research Establishment are available through Her Majesty's Stationery Office, Government bookshops or through any bookseller.

Building Centres

These are information centres which deal with all aspects of the construction industry and are situated in the main centres of population such as London, Birmingham, Bristol, Cambridge, Glasgow, Liverpool, Manchester, Nottingham and Southampton. Together with the Building Information Centres at Coventry, Durham and Stoke-on-Trent, they provide a complete network of centres to which the designer can apply for quick and full answers to queries and problems on materials, products, services and techniques.

Much of the information given either verbally or by issuing literature is free, but information which necessitates search processes is carried out by the Technical Research Service (FIND) for which a fee is charged. Most centres also operate a Data Express Service which is operated through the main centre in London to provide a fast first-class post literature distribution service for trade and professional enquiries. Other functions carried out by building centres are exhibitions, meetings, conference and trade receptions which enables a great deal of information to be publicised and exchanged.

Agrément Certificates

These are issued by the Agrément Board which has its headquarters and testing unit at the Building Research Station. The Agrément Board is mainly concerned with the impartial assessment of new materials, components and systems which are not covered by a British Standard. The testing and assessment is carried out by request from the manufacturer, who supplies all the required data to the board which institutes the necessary tests in the context of purpose, suitability, safety and durability for an agreed fee.

If the board's conclusions are satisfactory, a certificate is issued which identifies the product, describes its use, gives constructional details together with the method of assembly or fixing. These certificates are a means of enabling the designer to assess if the new product would be suitable for incorporation into his design.

Research and development associations

These bodies are normally concerned with research and development in a particular material or method of construction and publish their findings in the form of data sheets, handbooks, textbooks and general information literature. The whole list of such associations is too lengthy to enumerate in a text of this nature but the topics covered range from agricultural buildings, ceramics, cement and concrete, copper, mastic asphalt, lead, paint, rubber, plastics, structural steelwork, timber research and development to transport and road research. A great deal of the information issued by these bodies is free but extensive publications are subject to a fee. Most of the research and development associations also organize courses, conferences, seminars and site visits to enable the information and services they have to offer to become widely known.

Manufacturers' information

The information obtainable from manufacturers is usually in one of three formats:

1. General: this is in the form of illustrated literature setting out basically the use and purpose of the product, very often listing successful designs in which the product has been incorporated.

2. Detailed: this is mainly presented in the form of a handbook giving full details of the properties, assembly or fixing and normally gives the designer all the technical data he needs. Other forms of presentation are data sheets and comprehensive catalogues or pamphlets.

3. Technical representatives: these are qualified persons trained in the use and design of the product who give advice and guidance to the designer especially when the design is special or is an out of the ordinary problem.

It should be noted that many manufacturers will provide a complete design service which may also include site work by their own trained staff.

The information is obtained from the manufacturers by direct application or by using the prepaid service cards included in most technical journals in which the manufacturer advertises. The initial enquiry usually results in general information literature being sent. Detailed information – which is more expensive to produce – can be forwarded to the designer should this be requested. Much of the information literature quoted above can be found in the various catalogue libraries.

Libraries and other sources

Many colleges of further education, polytechnics, universities and professional institutes have special libraries or sections of libraries devoted entirely to all kinds of information relating to the construction industry including manufacturers' literature, British Standards, Building Research Establishment and Her Majesty's Stationery Office publications together with articles which have appeared in the various journals and magazines, all filed under the CI/SfB system.

This system classifies information under various headings called tables:

1. *Table 0 – Physical Environment:* basically this refers to the end product.

2. *Table 1 – Elements:* such as walls, floors, ceilings and services.

3. *Table 2 – Construction Forms:* such as brick, block pipes and tiles.

4. *Table 3 – Materials:* this is a large section dealing specifically with all forms of materials ranging from natural stone to paints.

5. *Table 5 – Activities and Requirements:* this section applies to anything which results from the building process and includes such items as management, plant, fire, maintenance and economics.

Other sources of information which may well be contained within a building reference library or section are:

1. *Barbour Index:* this is an integrated library of product information intended primarily for architects and quantity surveyors and is available to subscribers. The library is presented in binders classified by CI/SfB and is kept up to date by a monthly visit by a Barbour Index representative. The types of information contained within each library can be at the customer's request and this is reviewed annually. Barbour Index Limited also offer the Barbour Design Library which consists of a library of some 45 000 pages of information stored on microfiche film which can be read through an illuminated screen reader. The library is up-dated three times a year and contains a vast store of information including all relevant British Standards and research organizations' data.

2. *RIBA Service Ltd: Product Data:* this is a subscribers' system comprising ten binders which contain concise factual data sheets on the products of some 550 manufacturers and these sheets are classified by CI/SfB and up-dated at regular intervals.

3. *Building Products Index:* this is another subscriber system similar in content and presentation to the Barbour Index system described above and contains data on the products of some 1250 manufacturers.

4. *Architects Standard Catalogue:* this is the oldest of the subscriber libraries, consisting of six volumes classified by CI/SfB giving data on the products of many manufacturers.

The above named sources of information are not the only outlets available to the designer but are a selection of the types of services obtainable by architects, builders, surveyors, estimators and specifiers engaged in the design process.

Access for maintenance

During the design period and the preparation of details the designer must be conscious of the need to make provision for maintenance by providing adequate access to hidden works such as services. Failure to provide the necessary access in the form of ducts, removable covers or trunking can have costly repercussions, since it would be:

(a) difficult to locate actual position of fault;
(b) necessary to remove or damage other parts of the structure to obtain access;
(c) elevating the cost of maintenance by adding both labour and material costs in making good damage to the fabric or structure;
(d) possible to cause disruption to other services whilst investigating the location of the fault in the service under consideration;
(e) possible to cause disruption to the general circulation within the building whilst exploratory and repair work is carried out.

The services within a building can constitute a large percentage of the total cost of building work, ranging from some 20 per cent in domestic work to as much as 60 per cent where complex services are involved. By careful design, planning and routing of the services the designer can achieve speed and continuity during the construction period, ease of maintenance, reduction in noise levels of services in operation, better protection from damage and generally easing the problems encountered when considering an extension to the services. To achieve these objectives the designer should consider the services aspect at an early stage in the design process. Guidance as to the minimum and optimum requirements for service ducts can be obtained from manufacturers, specialist engineers and publications such as CP 413: Ducts for Building Services.

Types of duct

The type of duct and its physical construction will depend upon three main factors, namely:

1. Size of the pipe or cable.
2. Direction and routing of the service.
3. Nature of service being conveyed.

Small services may well only require a simple recess whereas large diameter services may require a duct large enough to give unimpeded access for maintenance personnel. The direction will have some bearing on the way in which the services are supported and the provision for movement of both services and maintenance personnel. The nature of the services being conveyed will dictate which services can be sited within the same duct, adjacent to one another, the need for insulation and/or ventilation and the degree of exposure permitted. The relationships of the different types of services to each other are set out in Table III of CP 413.

Small services: these may be considered as those below 65 mm diameter and can be run either vertically or horizontally housed in floor or wall recesses,

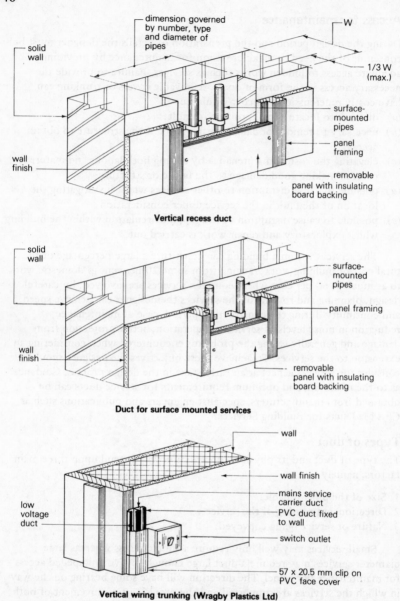

Fig. 2.5. Typical vertical ducts for small services

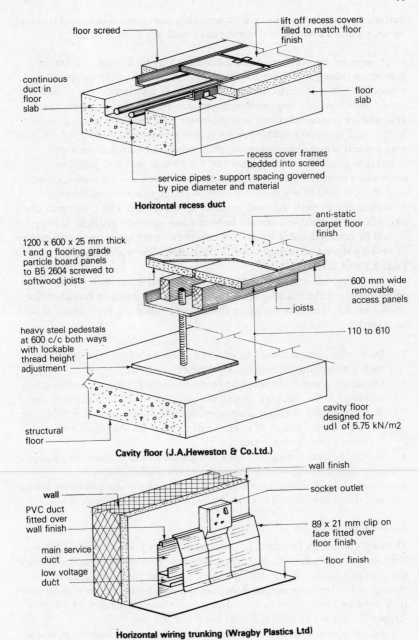

Horizontal recess duct

floor screed

lift off recess covers
filled to match floor
finish

continuous
duct in
floor
slab

floor
slab

recess cover frames
bedded into screed

service pipes - support spacing governed
by pipe diameter and material

1200 x 600 x 25 mm thick
t and g flooring grade
particle board panels
to BS 2604 screwed to
softwood joists

anti-static
carpet floor
finish

600 mm wide
removable
access panels

joists

heavy steel pedestals
at 600 c/c both ways
with lockable
thread height
adjustment

110 to 610

structural
floor

cavity floor
designed for
udl of 5.75 kN/m2

Cavity floor (J.A.Heweston & Co.Ltd.)

wall finish

wall

PVC duct
fitted over
wall finish

main service
duct

low voltage
duct

socket outlet

89 x 21 mm clip on
face fitted over
floor finish

floor finish

Horizontal wiring trunking (Wragby Plastics Ltd)

Fig. 2.6. Typical horizontal ducts for small services

surface mounted with a suitable removable cover, housed in special trunking or situated in a cavity floor. For typical details see Figs. 2.5 and 2.6.

Large services: services over 65 mm diameter may be housed in a similar manner to those given above for small services but when the complexity, number and sizes increase, horizontal subway or crawlway ducts should be considered. Similarly large vertical ducts with floor or ladder access can be designed for the complex and large diameter services. Subway ducts should have a clear minimum working space of 700 mm wide × 2000 mm high with general access from basement, plant room or control room with removable access covers of at least 450 × 600 mm plan size positioned at convenient points, especially at changes of direction and junctions. Crawl-way ducts should have a clear minimum working space of 700 mm wide × 1000 mm high with removable access covers at least 450 × 600 mm plan size situated at suitable intervals. In both cases adequate artificial lighting should be installed and if the duct is situated in waterlogged ground a system of tanking should be incorporated in the design. For typical details see Figs. 2.7 and 2.8.

The interconnection of horizontal and vertical ducts with one another and throughout the building can create a fire risk in terms of spread of fire and/or smoke; therefore to reduce this risk the following precautions should be taken:

1. Duct construction should be of non-combustible materials throughout with a minimum fire resistance period of one hour.
2. Openings in the duct should be confined to pipe inlets or outlets which will require fire stopping around the pipe where it passes through the duct fabric and to access door openings, the door of which should have a fire resistance period of at least half an hour and be fitted with an automatic self-closing device.
3. Where the duct passes through a fire-resistant wall or floor, fire stopping should be placed between the duct and the wall or floor.
4. Vertical ducts should have a vent at the top of the shaft to allow smoke and flame to escape in the event of a fire penetrating the duct.

Suspended ceilings

The void created by this form of construction may provide an ideal housing for horizontal services which can be supported from the structural slab above the void and hidden by the ceiling below. Wherever these services pass through a fire-resistant wall or floor, like those in horizontal or vertical ducts, they must be fire stopped in accordance with the requirements of Building Regulation E 14. For typical details see Fig. 2.9.

All services should be easily identifiable to ease the problems of repair and maintenance. The recommendations in BS 1710 – Specification for Identification of Pipe Lines – should be followed. This standard recommends a system of colour coding with symbols and abbreviations where appropriate.

The contents of this chapter have been to show the importance of the

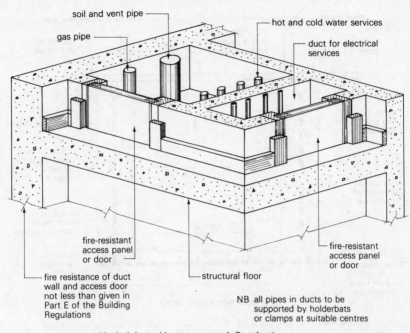

soil and vent pipe ⎯

hot and cold water services

gas pipe ⎯

⎯ duct for electrical services

fire-resistant access panel or door ⎯

⎯ fire-resistant access panel or door

⎯ fire resistance of duct wall and access door not less than given in Part E of the Building Regulations

⎯ structural floor

NB all pipes in ducts to be supported by holderbats or clamps at suitable centres

Vertical duct with access at each floor level

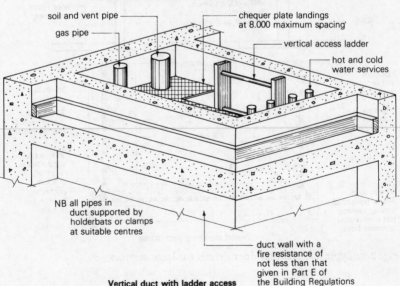

soil and vent pipe ⎯

⎯ chequer plate landings at 8.000 maximum spacing

gas pipe ⎯

⎯ vertical access ladder

⎯ hot and cold water services

NB all pipes in duct supported by holderbats or clamps at suitable centres

⎯ duct wall with a fire resistance of not less than that given in Part E of the Building Regulations

Vertical duct with ladder access

Fig. 2.7. Typical vertical duct details for large services

50

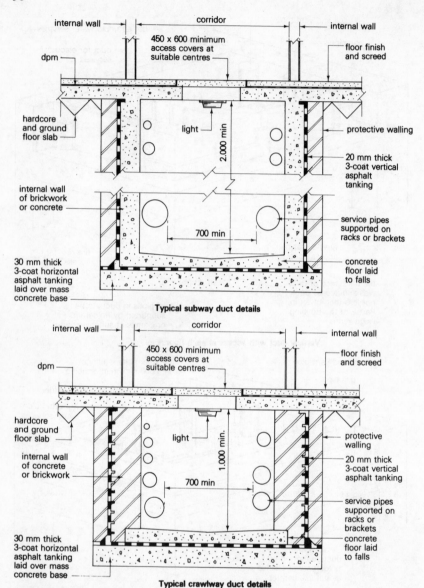

Typical subway duct details

Typical crawlway duct details

Fig. 2.8. Typical horizontal duct details for large services

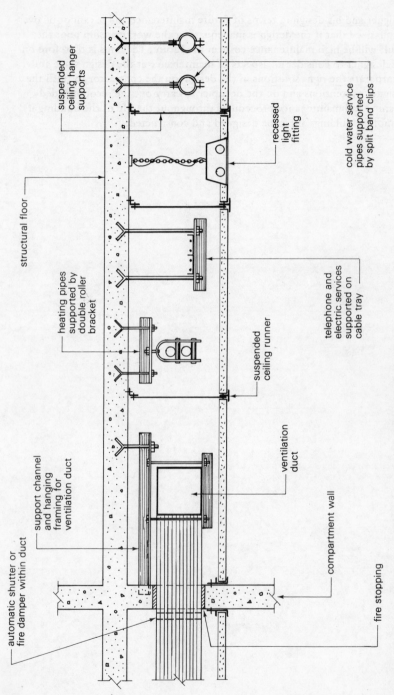

Fig. 2.9. Typical details of services housed in suspended ceiling void

suspended ceiling hanger supports

recessed light fitting

cold water service pipes supported by split band clips

structural floor

heating pipes supported by double roller bracket

suspended ceiling runner

telephone and electric services supported on cable tray

ventilation duct

support channel and hanging framing for ventilation duct

compartment wall

automatic shutter or fire damper within duct

fire stopping

designer and his design in terms of future maintenance and it cannot be over-emphasized that if the design is inadequate or the workmanship poor the result will be high maintenance costs in the future. The onus is therefore on the designer to consider all aspects of maintenance at the design stage and incorporate the right solutions in the design, on the contractor to fulfil the designer's intentions and on the occupier to carry out the recommended cleaning and maintenance procedures throughout the life of the building if economic buildings are to be designed and constructed.

Chapter 3

Economic considerations

The useful life of a property will be governed by a number of factors ranging from the extent to which maintenance was considered and included in the design, the degree to which the occupier carries out maintenance work during the life of the building and economic considerations. There will come a time in the life of any property when the decision will have to be taken as to whether the building should continue to be maintained or adapted to a more suitable usage, since the only alternative to these options is to demolish and rebuild.

A building can be considered as having three distinct lives, namely:

1. Physical life: assuming the property is structurally sound, this life can be extended almost indefinitely by careful maintenance.

2. Functional life: a property may no longer fulfil its original functional intention due to social and technological changes; however, it may be possible to adapt the building to cater for these changes or alternatively adapt it for a different usage.

3. Economic life: a comparison of costs of maintaining a property against replacement is usually the best indicator of economic viability, but in some cases the economic life may be geared to the value of the site on which the building is situated.

Physical life

All buildings wear out because the materials of which they are composed have an estimated life expectancy and combinations of these materials will in turn impart a life expectancy to the elements they constitute. To assess the actual life of any particular material or element is not an easy task since this life expectancy will depend on a number of factors such as the original material specification, the design of components where materials are working in conjunction with one another, the effects of weathering and the location of the building under consideration.

The best method of estimating the life expectancy is to take as a base figures obtained from acceptable sources such as research results and manufacturers' data and adjust these figures by past experience and feedback information. The results can then be tabulated or presented in the form of a bar chart to give an overall assessment of life expectancy and thus enable maintenance cycles to be projected. For a typical bar chart example see Fig. 3.1.

A bar chart or table similar to that shown in Fig. 3.1 should be prepared, by means of a detailed investigation and study, as soon as practicable after occupation of the property. This will enable both resources and finances to be planned and projected from the outset. The bar chart or table will need to be reviewed and amended in the light of experience; for example, it may be found by the passage of time that the external decoration needs to be carried out every four years and not every five years as originally predicted. It can be seen from Fig. 3.1 that the life of the hypothetical building under review will start to become critical after the eightieth year, since with only ten years of its life expectancy to run it may not be an economical proposition to carry out the maintenance cycles on other elements such as the rainwater goods.

Functional life

All buildings are designed for a specific function or usage: changes in technology, social needs and/or mode of living can make the property inadequate, unacceptable or non-competitive. Numerous examples can be quoted but a few will serve to illustrate the point.

Shops

The tendency in recent years has been to change from a system of counters separating the customer from the items for sale and the assistant, to open planning with a self-service approach with cash or pay points at strategic positions within the shop. Many shop premises can be converted to this style of business, but coupled with the self-service aspect has been the growth from the small-unit shops to the larger department stores and supermarkets for which the older style small-unit shop premises are not suitable for conversion or adaptation.

Hotels

Higher affluence, speed and ease of travel has promoted a rapid growth in the tourist industry, particularly in the field of package holidays, many of which do not include meals within the package. This in turn has led to many hotels becoming a collection of bedrooms with only the minimum facilities

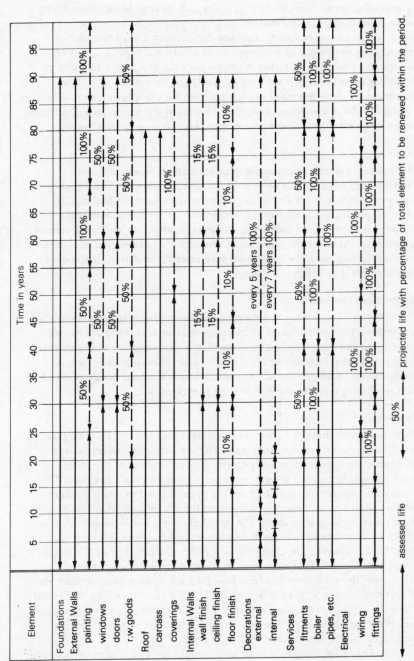

Fig. 3.1. Life expectancy for a building in terms of renewal cycles

for providing meals. The old style of hotel with its large lounges and dining rooms is becoming less fashionable, and since such facilities cannot be readily converted into extra bedroom accommodation, they are often under-utilized. The preference of many people to a cafeteria type of service has also led to a change in emphasis in the preparation and service required in the dining rooms of hotels catering primarily for the tourist. The above comments are more relevant to hotels catering for the tourist who is only staying for one or two nights before moving on to the next stop, rather than the hotel which caters for the tourist who stays for one or more weeks.

Factories

Rapid changes in manufacturing techniques both in production and assembly tend to make this form of building reach the end of its designed functional life in a much shorter period than other forms of building. In factories, production areas, layout and circulation are paramount if the company is to produce a commodity at an economic cost which will remain competitive; therefore the question of adaptation or demolition with subsequent rebuilding has to be considered very carefully and at more frequent intervals than that of other buildings.

Theatres and cinemas

The high cost of mounting and running the production coupled with the competition from other forms of entertainment such as television has led generally to the need for theatres of smaller seating capacity and to cinemas being sub-divided into two or three smaller units. Theatres and cinemas which cannot be adapted or where the demand is low have no alternative but to close, having come to the end of their functional life.

Dwellings

These have gone through a great many changes over the last 100 years due mainly to social and economic factors. The big Victorian houses built to accommodate large families with a staff of servants dictated the format of many rooms over several storeys, each room having an open fireplace. This format is no longer functional due to the present trend of much smaller families, which in turn eliminates the need for a large number of rooms and the servants to look after them. The population as a whole has gained more affluence and therefore demands a higher standard of living accommodation than that provided by the classic two-up and two-down type of Victorian house built for the lower paid workers. Many couples today opt for a marriage without children and therefore they are seeking much smaller units of accommodation which can be provided by flats as opposed to traditional houses. The larger Victorian properties which are no longer functional can very often be adapted to meet this demand. The same argument can be applied to the requirements of the single person.

The change in living habits has also brought about a change in functional design and layout of housing schemes. The dependence of many people on convenience foods has meant in many cases the decrease in importance of the traditional space for a vegetable or kitchen garden, and this, together with the general rise in the population over the last few decades, has led to an increase in the density of housing schemes. Health education has also played its part in the basic requirements such as internal toilets and bathrooms; this, coupled with the large increase in the number of private motor cars needing parking or garage space, has reduced the functional aspects of many older dwellings in terms of today's mode of living. Whether these properties can be adapted to fulfil a present-day function can only be assessed by considering each dwelling on its own merit.

Economic life

Before considering the economic life of a building the term 'economic' should be defined. Economic is the adjective of the noun economy, which may be defined as management of a household and its affairs, wise expenditure of money, careful use of materials and harmonious organization. It can therefore be seen that economics does not deal solely with the monetary aspects although this does form an important part of any consideration when assessing the economic life of a building.

In building terms the most important and indeed the first decision to be taken is the decision to carry out building work, whether it be new construction, adaptation or maintenance. This initial decision will be followed by the general management pattern of appraisal of what, when, where and how? What work is to be carried out? When is it to be done? Where should or can it be carried out? How should it be done? The initial decision must come from the client and in the case of a dwelling it is generally a simple matter governed usually by his financial situation and any particular personal preferences. However, companies, local authorities and government departments may well be faced with possible alternatives such as the provision of a new assembly shop as against an increased storage area. Priorities and benefits may well be governing factors but economic decisions based on investment, return on capital outlay and cost-in-use appraisals may well be of paramount importance.

The techniques which can be employed to assess the economic life of a building were introduced in principle in Chapter 1. A complete detailed study of the various methods of ascertaining the feasibility of a project or proposal are beyond the scope of this text but a basic appreciation of the most common methods used is within the syllabus of the course on which this book is based. The technique by which most of these assessment studies is carried out is called discounting, which was briefly defined in Chapter 1 as a method of calculating the present value of a sum of money due in the future. The reason for using discounting techniques is to bring all the moneys involved in the project or proposal to a common base which is usually taken as today or its present value since moneys which are received or paid out at different times will have different values. It should also be remembered that discounting is basically the reciprocal of compounding (see Ch. 1). Discounting factors are usually obtained from books of valuation tables and where necessary the relevant factors have been reproduced to enable the reader to follow the examples.

Two simple examples should be sufficient to show the value of discounting to a present-day value.

Example 1
Consideration is to be given to three alternatives for a project with an anticipated life of forty years.

Project 1	Capital outlay	£5000
	Maintenance	£200 in 15 years.
Project 2	Capital outlay	£5000
	Maintenance	£100 in 20 years
		£125 in 30 years.
Project 3	Capital outlay	£5000
	Maintenance	£100 in 15 years
		£150 in 35 years.

If a comparison is made in terms of cash outlay:

Project 1 costs £5000 + £200 = £5200
Project 2 costs £5000 + £225 = £5225
Project 3 costs £5000 + £250 = £5250

but to obtain a true comparison the maintenance moneys to be paid in the future should be discounted to a present-day value or, in other words, what sum of money must be invested now to realize the maintenance sum due in the future? Assume discounting rate to be 7 per cent.

Project 1: amount to be invested today at 7 per cent compound interest
to yield £200 in fifteen years' time
= capital × discount factor (from tables)
= £200 × 0.3624
= £72.48

Project 2: £100 × 0.2584 = 25.84
£125 × 0.1314 = 16.43
total   = £42.27

Project 3: £100 × 0.3624 = 36.24
£150 × 0.0937 = 14.05
total   = £50.29

Therefore the present-day cash outlay for each project is:

Project 1 £5000 + £72.48 = £5072.48
Project 2 £5000 + £42.27 = £5042.27
Project 3 £5000 + £50.29 = £5050.29

From the simple example above it can be seen that in terms of total capital outlay Project 1 is the most advantageous, whereas when compared with discounting to present-day values Project 2 is in fact the most advantageous and Project 1 is the worst of the three examples.

Example 2

Consideration is to be given to three proposals for replacing an existing glazed door and frame with an anticipated life of thirty years. Assume discounting rate to be 6 per cent.

Proposal 1 –   softwood glazed door and frame including fixing with maintenance required every five years at a cost of £25.00.

Proposal 2 –   hardwood glazed door and frame including fixing with maintenance required every 6 years at a cost of £15.00.

Proposal 3 –   aluminium alloy glazed door and frame including fixing with no maintenance required.

Discounting factors (from valuation tables)

Years	Factor
5	0.7473
6	0.7050
10	0.5584
12	0.4970
15	0.4173
18	0.3503
20	0.3118
24	0.2470
25	0.2330

Proposal 1. Capital cost = £40.00

    Maintenance   5th year = 0.7473
                    10th year = 0.5584
                    15th year = 0.4173
                    20th year = 0.3118
                    25th year = 0.2330

$$2.2678 \times 25 = £56.70$$
$$\text{present-day value} = £96.70$$

Proposal 2. Capital cost = £95.00

    Maintenance   6th year = 0.7050
                    12th year = 0.4970
                    18th year = 0.3503
                    24th year = 0.2470

$$1.7993 \times 15 = £26.99$$
$$\text{present-day value} = £121.99$$

Proposal 3. Capital cost = £145.00

    Maintenance =   nil
                    present-day value   = £145.00

From the above it can be concluded that the most economic proposal in terms of capital outlay and maintenance costs is Proposal 1.

It should be noted that in the above examples inflation trends have been ignored, since this would be a common factor. Taxation implications regarding maintenance have also been ignored as these can fluctuate according to government policy, and since it is the basic conception of discounting techniques which are being considered, the inclusion of such figures may lead to confusion. It should also be noted that in Example 2 the discounting factors were summated before being multiplied by the periodic maintenance cost. This is only possible where such a cost is a constant, otherwise each cost must be calculated separately as shown in Example 1.

The above examples have both been concerned only with outgoings, no account having been taken of any earnings. In Example 2 there would not of course have been any return and therefore the example is a practicable exercise, but in Example 1 there could well have been a monetary return and this should be taken into account when considering the economics of a proposal.

The discounting methods available to take into account both outgoings and incomings are:

1. *Net present value:* this is the difference between the discounted value of all net income and initial outlay over the life of the building.

2. *Equivalent annual value:* this is the amount which if paid annually over the life of the project would be equal to the present-day value of the net income.

3. *Internal rate of return:* this is the rate of return expressed as a percentage per annum that can be obtained from the project over its whole life after deducting all outgoings.

The following examples should illustrate the use of the above discounting methods.

Example 1   *Net present value*
Proposal A
Capital outlay = £25 000.00
Net income = rent – (maintenance + operating costs)
Discounting rate = 8 per cent

Year	Net income (£)	Discounting factor	Present-day value (£)
1	7500	0.9259	6944.25
2	8000	0.9573	6858.40
3	8500	0.7938	6747.30
4	9000	0.7350	6615.00
5	10 000	0.6806	6806.00
6	9500	0.6302	5986.90

Year	Net income (£)	Discounting factor	Present-day value (£)
7	8750	0.5835	5105.63
8	8250	0.5403	4457.48
9	7000	0.5002	3501.40
10	6000	0.4632	2779.20

total = 82 500   total = 55 801.56

– capital outlay   25 000.00

net present value = £30 801.56

Proposal B
Capital outlay = £37 500
Discounting rate = 8 per cent

Year	Net Income (£)	Discounting factor	Present-day value (£)
1	9750	0.9259	9027.53
2	10 000	0.8573	8573.00
3	10 500	0.7938	8334.90
4	10 800	0.7350	7938.00
5	11 000	0.6806	7486.60
6	10 600	0.6302	6680.12
7	10 500	0.5835	6126.75
8	9800	0.5403	5294.94
9	9700	0.5002	4851.94
10	9500	0.4632	4400.40

total = 102 150   total = 68 714.18

– capital outlay   37 500.00

net present value = £31 214.18

It can clearly be seen that both Proposals A and B are profitable since the net present value in both cases is greater than zero and that Proposal B seems to be better than Proposal A since the net present value is higher for the same life span, but the capital outlay for Proposal B is one and a half times that of Proposal A; however, the net present value of Proposal B is not one and a half times the capital outlay, therefore, on this basis of comparison, Proposal A would be the most economical investment.

Example 2 *Equivalent annual value*
Proposal A as set out above in the net present value example has a net present value of £30 801.56. The present value of £1 per annum for ten years at 8 per

cent rate of interest = £6.71 (this figure is taken from valuation tables giving the present value of one pound per annum which gives the factor by which future annual payments must be multiplied to obtain the present-day value).

Proposal A
Equivalent annual value

$$= \frac{\text{net present value}}{\text{present value of £1 per annum}}$$

$$= \frac{30\ 801.56}{6.71}$$

$$= £4590.40$$

Proposal B
Equivalent annual value

$$= \frac{\text{net present value}}{\text{present value of £1 per annum}}$$

$$= \frac{31\ 214.18}{6.71}$$

$$= £4651.89$$

The above results again show profitability for both proposals; indeed, since the time factor is the same in both cases the results should give exactly the same indication as the net present value method. If the equivalent annual value had been less than zero the proposals would have been costing more than they received in income. The equivalent annual value figure tells us that if the net present value in Proposal A of £30 801.56 was invested at 8 per cent compound interest it would enable an annual payment of £4590.40 to be made throughout the life of the proposal starting at the end of the first year. The invested capital would be decreased by £4590.40 each year to leave a zero balance after the payment at the end of the tenth year.

Example 3 *Internal rate of return*
This is sometimes called the discounted cash flow rate of return and can be found by trial and error using valuation tables to find the rate which will discount the net income so that the total value of the discounted net income is nearly equal to the original cost. The alternative to trial and error methods, which can be time consuming and laborious, is to use a suitable computer program. By trial and error the internal rates of return for Proposals A and B in the previous examples were found to be 31 and 24 per cent respectively as shown below and by computer the internal rates of return were given as 30.9819 and 24.168 per cent respectively.

The discounting methods set out above and below are techniques which can be applied to any form of building whether it is a new structure, adaptation, extension or merely a replacement or repair item to assess the viability of a proposal or project. It should now be clear that any method which uses discounting techniques is better than any method which does noi Whichever method is chosen the conclusion reached should be the same, however, the internal rate of return method is favoured by many people who have to take the final decision on whether and how to expend capital on a proposal or project since it will show the yield, which is one of the prime concerns of anyone in business.

Proposal A

Year	Net income (£)	Discounting factor (31%)	Discounted value (£)
1	7500	0.7634	5725.50
2	8000	0.5827	4661.60
3	8500	0.4448	3780.80
4	9000	0.3396	3056.40
5	10 000	0.2592	2592.00
6	9500	0.1979	1880.05
7	8750	0.1510	1321.25
8	8250	0.1153	951.23
9	7000	0.0880	616.00
10	6000	0.0672	403.20

total discounted value = £24 988.03

original cost = £25 000.00

Proposal B

Year	Net income (£)	Discounting factor (24%)	Discounted value (£)
1	9750	0.8065	7863.38
2	10 000	0.6504	6504.00
3	10 500	0.5245	5507.25
4	10 800	0.4230	4568.40
5	11 000	0.3411	3752.10
6	10 600	0.2751	2916.06
7	10 500	0.2218	2328.90
8	9800	0.1789	1753.22
9	9700	0.1443	1399.71
10	9500	0.1164	1105.80

total discounted value = £37 698.82

original cost = £37 500.00

Provided that the interest rate at which money can be borrowed is less than the internal rate of return the proposals are profitable, in the above example Proposal A is more favourable than Proposal B.

Cost-in-use

The object of a cost-in-use study is to determine the method of fulfilling a certain building requirement at the least total cost. To find the total cost of a building over its anticipated life the following must be taken into account:

1. *Capital cost:* the total initial cost of the project.

2. *Operating costs:* this would include all outgoings necessary to service the building such as heat, light, power, management, insurances and all necessary attendant labour resources.

3. *Maintenance costs:* this would include all necessary expenditure in repairing and renewing all parts of the structure, services and finishes.

The total cost is the summation of the three items listed above and since all these costs will occur at different times they will need to be discounted at their net present value, or alternatively their equivalent annual value, as shown in the following example:

Proposal 1

Discounting rate	= 8 per cent
Capital costs	= £25 000
Operating costs	= £2125 per annum
Maintenance costs	= £1750 per annum
Life of proposal	= 20 years

Combined operating and maintenance costs = £2125 + £1750 = £3875 per annum.

From valuation tables of the present value of one pound per annum:

£3875 for 20 years	= 3875 × 9.8181
	= £38 045.14
total cost of proposal	= £25 000 + £38 045.14
	= £63 045.14

Proposal 2

Discounting rate	= 8 per cent
Capital cost	= £23 400
Operating costs	= £2 000 per annum
Maintenance costs	= £1600 per annum
Replacement cost 1	= £750 in year 10
Replacement cost 2	= £500 in year 15
Life of proposal	= 20 years

Combined operating and maintenance cost = £2000 + £1600 = £3600 per annum.

From valuation tables present values are:

£3600 for 20 years	= 3600 × 9.8181	= 35 345.16
£750 in 10 years	= 750 × 0.4632	= 347.40
£500 in 15 years	= 500 × 0.3152	= 157.60
	total	= 35 850.16
total cost of proposal	= £23 400 + £35 850.16	
	= £59 250.16	

The above cost-in-use studies show that Proposal 2 has the lower present-day value and on this basis should be adopted. If the net incomes for the two proposals were identical in all respects the study would also be a test for profitability, but if the net incomes differed, which is usually the case, then an internal rate of return or discounted cash flow assessment should be carried out to ascertain the respective yields of the proposals.

Cost-in-use techniques are simple to use and give the design team and the client a clear indication of the economics of the proposal or proposals over the life of the project rather than immediate capital outlay considerations. The limitation of this form of appraisal lies in the difficulty of forecasting trends in costs such as a change in the interest rate or shortfall in anticipated income when calculating the internal rate of return. The latter consideration can be included in any complete study by taking into account sensitivity as shown in the example given in Chapter 1, but the method of carrying out such calculations are beyond the scope of this text.

Repair or replacement decisions

Very often the question arises during the life of a building as to whether it is more economical to repair an item or component than to replace it. Generally it can be assumed that the anticipated life of a replacement would be greater than that of carrying out repairs or remedial treatment to the existing item. If this is the case a simple calculation will show the maximum amount which can be expended on the repair work before it becomes uneconomic.

Example 1

Let £x = repair cost
  £y = replacement cost
  8% = interest rate
estimated life of repair   = 10 years
estimated life of replacement   = 20 years
Equivalent annual value of repair = $\dfrac{x}{6.7101}$

Equivalent annual value of replacement = $\dfrac{y}{9.8181}$

(The denominations in the above fractions are taken from valuation tables giving the present value of one pound per annum.)

for x and y to be equal

$$\frac{x}{6.7101} = \frac{y}{9.8181}$$

$$x = \frac{6.7101\,y}{9.8181}$$

$$= 0.6834\,y$$

This means that it would be uneconomic to carry out a repair if its cost was more than 68.34 per cent of a replacement cost. Therefore if replacement costs were £250.00 then it would be uneconomic to carry out repairs if the cost exceeded 68.34 per cent of £250.00 = £170.85.

Example 2

Let £x = repair cost
£y = replacement cost
9% = interest rate

| estimated life of repair | = | 5 years |
| estimated life of replacement | = | 25 years |

Equivalent annual value of repair $= \dfrac{x}{3.8897}$

Equivalent annual value of replacement $= \dfrac{y}{9.8226}$

for x and y to be equal

$$\frac{x}{3.8897} = \frac{y}{9.8226}$$

$$x = \frac{3.8897\,y}{9.8226}$$

$$= 0.396\,y$$

In this case it would be uneconomic to carry out a repair if its cost was more than 39.6 per cent of a replacement cost. It should also be noted that the higher the rate of interest the greater will be the amount which can be expended on repair work even taking into account the shorter life. In the case of Example 2 above the increase in the percentage of replacement cost with the increase in interest rates would be as follows:

10% = 41.76%
12% = 46.67%
15% = 51.86%

The above examples do not take into account any benefit which may be gained by a replacement in terms of greater efficiency or lower operation costs due to technological advances.

Example 3

The decision has to be taken whether to replace a component at a cost of £1650 with an annual operating cost of £275 with an anticipated life of twenty-five years or whether to repair the existing component at a cost of £950 with an annual operating cost of £320 to extend its life by twelve years.

Replacement
Equivalent annual cost of £1650 over twenty-five years at 8 per cent

$$= \frac{1650}{10.6748} \qquad = 154.60$$

annual operating cost   = 275.00

total annual cost   = 429.60

Repair
Equivalent annual cost of £950 over twelve years at 8 per cent

$$= \frac{950}{7.5361} = 126.06$$

annual operating cost   = 320.00

total annual cost   =£446.06

The above comparison indicates that a replacement would be the most economical course of action. The above examples have been calculated using the equivalent annual cost method which is usually preferred by tenants and maintenance managers since they are primarily concerned with annual costs, whereas designers, who are primarily concerned with capital outlay, would normally use the net present value method as shown below:

Replacement
Capital cost   = £1650.00
Present value of £275 for 25 years = 275 × 10.6748   = £2935.57
                                        total cost   = £4585.57

Repair
Capital cost   = £950.00
Present value of £320 for 12 years = 320 × 7.5361   = £2411.55
                                        total cost   = £3361.55

This comparison, due to the different time factors, indicates the opposite economic appraisal to that of the equivalent annual cost, but it does not take into account that at the end of twelve years further expenditure will be needed either to repair or replace the component in question.

Repairs and dilapidations

The study of the legal and economic implications of the want of repair and the question of dilapidations is complex and it is not intended under this heading to analyse deeply the legal aspects involved since it is not required by the syllabus which forms the basis of this text. In the context of the heading, consideration will be given to the relationship between landlord and tenant with regard to their respective responsibilities to repairs and dilapidations, enabling accurate economic assessments to be made.

When an agreement has been reached between a landlord and tenant a relationship has been established between them by a contract of tenancy called a lease, letting or demise. A contract is an agreement between two or more persons which creates rights and duties enforceable by action at law. The liability for repairs is usually set out in the lease and these will vary considerably according to the type of property and the purpose for which it has been let. Under the Law of Property Act 1925 the law requires a deed for all leases which are granted for a period exceeding three years; for lettings of less duration written leases are not legally required, but it is usual for a written agreement to be prepared setting out the terms agreed between landlord and tenant.

Primarily the liability of landlord and tenant for repairs are in the terms of the contract of tenancy but, if not, some covenants are implied by law. As a general rule a landlord is under no obligation whatsoever to a tenant in respect of the physical state of the premises or indeed its suitability for the intended usage at the commencement of the tenancy, with the following exceptions:

1. *New houses:* it has always been the rule at common law that a builder who sells a house to be completed is under an implied obligation that the house will be fit for human habitation upon completion unless there is agreement to the contrary (*Perry* v *Sharon Development Co* (1937)).

2. *Small houses at low rents:* by Section 6 of the Housing Act 1957 there is an implied condition that the house is at the commencement and during the tenancy kept fit by the landlord for human habitation. The low rents referred to are not exceeding £80 a year in the administrative county of London and £52 elsewhere and refer to the letting of a house or part of a house. Where the contract of letting was between 6 July 1957 and 1 April 1965, before this period the low rents were half those quoted above. This does not apply if the house is let for three years or more and the tenant agrees to make it habitable and the lease cannot be determined before the end of three years.

3. *Furnished houses:* there is at common law an implied undertaking on the part of the landlord that at the time of letting the premises are reasonably fit for human habitation (*Smith* v *Marrable* (1843)) but there is no implied obligation on the landlord that the furnished house (or flat) shall continue to be fit for habitation during the term of the lease (*Sarson* v *Roberts* (1895)).

4. *New dwelling:* there is an implied obligation of fitness for habitation on the landlord if he was involved in the provision of the dwelling but not if it is covered by a National House-Builders Council certificate. (Section 1 Defective Premises Act 1972.)

Further to the above, a landlord is under no implied contractual obligation for repairs or maintenance during the course of a tenancy except for:

1. Small houses at low rents – as given in 2 above.
2. Dwellings let for a term of less than seven years – by Sections 32 and 33 of the Housing Act 1961 the implied contractual obligations are that the landlord will:

   (a) keep in repair the structure and exterior of the dwelling including drains, gutters and external pipes;

(*b*) keep in repair and proper working order the installations in the dwelling house for the supply of water, gas and electricity and for sanitation including basins, sinks and sanitary conveniences – but except those, not for fixtures, fittings and appliances for making use of the supply of water, gas or electricity.

The standard of upkeep demanded by the above implied contractual obligations depends on age, character, anticipated life and locality of the dwelling.

The implied contractual obligations on the landlord to carry out repairs and maintenance given above does not relieve the tenant of his repairing obligations of using the demised premises in a proper and tenant-like manner and to delivering up possession at the end of the tenancy in the same condition as when let, fair wear and tear excepted. The meaning of the term in a tenant-like manner is 'the tenant must take proper care of the place. He must, if he is going away for the winter, turn off the water and empty the boiler. He must clean the chimneys, when necessary, and also the windows. He must mend the electric light when it fuses. He must unstop the sink when it is blocked by his own waste. In short, he must do the little jobs about the place which a reasonable tenant would do. In addition, he must, of course, not damage the house, wilfully or negligently; and he must see that his family or guests do not damage it; and if they do, he must repair it. But apart from such things, if the house falls into disrepair through fair wear and tear or lapse of time, or for any reason not caused by him, then the tenant is not liable to repair it'. (*Warren* v *Keen* (1954).)

The term 'fair wear and tear' is an English idiom and is generally accepted as meaning that a tenant's liability for disrepair is excused if arising from the following causes:

1. Normal action of time and the elements such as wind and weather.
2. Normal and reasonable usage of the premises by the tenant for the purpose of the letting.

Tenants on a year-to-year tenancy are only liable to keep the premises wind and watertight and are not liable to do substantial repairs. (*Leach* v *Thomas* (1835).)

Where there is a general covenant to repair the following expressions may be used:

1. *To put into repair:* seldom imposed on the tenant but it is sometimes used when leased premises are let in a dilapidated condition with the intention that the tenant will repair and improve the property at his own expense. Sometimes the term 'necessary repair' is used and this means carrying out such repairs at the commencement of the tenancy, but the term 'forthwith' does not mean immediately but within a reasonable time and it would be for a jury to decide what, in any particular case, was reasonable.

2. *To keep in repair:* this creates an obligation for the duration of the lease to keep the premises in the same state as they were let and to deliver them up at

the end of the lease in a similar state. The term 'repair' will always indicate a certain amount of renewal since when carrying out repairs it is very often necessary to renew a part of the whole in order to effect the repair. A tenant who accepts such a covenant is bound to renew any parts that cannot be repaired but such a covenant will never extend to the rebuilding of the premises as a whole if caused by old age or defect. (*Lurcott* v *Wakeley and Wheeler* (1911).)

3. *Fair wear and tear excepted:* this will exclude the tenant from liability for dilapidations caused by normal and reasonable usage of the premises and the operation of external forces, but it will not excuse the tenant from the effects of damage flowing from the wear and tear. If a slate falls off through wear and tear and in consequence the roof is likely to let through water, the tenant is not responsible for the slate coming off, but he ought to put in another one to prevent further damage. (*Regis Property Co Ltd* v *Dudley* (1958).)

Standard of repair

If a building is in a dilapidated condition the standard of repair to be undertaken by the tenant under the terms of his covenant will vary according to circumstances but generally the premises must be kept in good tenantable repair. A good tenantable repair is such repairs as having regard to age, character and location as would make it reasonably fit for occupation by a reasonably minded tenant of the class who would be likely to take it. (*Proudfoot* v *Hart* (1890).)

Dilapidations

Where a tenant who has covenanted to keep the property in repair fails to do so, the landlord may always serve a notice upon him requiring him to repair, and where the lease is running out such notices are common. At the end of the lease if the tenant has failed to perform his obligations the landlord will require damages, and a surveyor is usually called in to prepare a schedule of dilapidations.

A schedule of dilapidations is a list of repairs rendered necessary by a tenant's neglect to carry out repairs as set out in the covenants of his lease. Schedules of dilapidations can take one of two forms:

1. *Interim schedule:* this consists of a list of defective items with a description of the necessary work which the tenant is required to have carried out in order to comply with the covenants in his lease and is limited to those items which are the tenant's responsibility. The schedule should mention every such item, it should also require him to restore everything which is missing but it should not require him to do the work in any definite manner. The wording of the schedule should avoid, wherever possible, technical terms so that it is easily understood by the tenant.

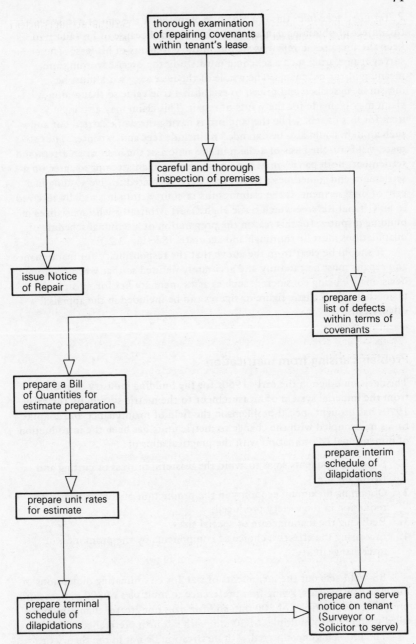

Fig. 3.2. Steps in preparing a schedule of dilapidations

2. Terminal schedule: this is a schedule prepared at the end of a lease with the object of obtaining damages from the tenant because of his failure to keep the premises in repair as set out in the covenants of his lease. The surveyor preparing such a schedule must study the precise wording and meaning of the covenants. The whole of the necessary work must be measured, described and priced to establish a true value so that a money claim may be made for the wants of repair. This claim may also include an item for loss of rent while the landlord is having the work carried out and such an item could also be extended to include fees and expenses. The estimate will form the basis of a claim in the action or the basis of an attempted settlement. Both parties may appoint surveyors in an attempt to agree on a settlement and sometimes a third party may be invited to give a ruling in a case of disagreement. If the claim results in court action it is usually referred to an Official Referee which is the High Court Arbitrator who specializes in building disputes; for this reason the preparation of a terminal schedule of dilapidations must be thorough and accurate. (See Fig. 3.2.)

It should be clear from the above that the responsibility for maintenance and repairs must be carefully and accurately defined so that when economic decisions are being considered, such as assessment studies for repairs and maintenance, a realistic figure or figures can be included in the appraisal calculations.

Problems arising from metrication

The decision taken in the early 1960s for the building industry to transfer from the imperial system of measurement to the metric system by the early 1970s has brought special problems in the field of maintenance and adaptation since coupled with the change to metric units has been the introduction of dimensional co-ordination with the practical aims of:

1. Sizing components so as to avoid the wasteful process of cutting and fitting on site.
2. Obtaining maximum economy in the production of components by a reduction in the variety produced.
3. Reducing the manufacture of special sizes.
4. Increasing the effective choice of components by the promotion of interchangeability.

BS 4011 sets out the increments of size for co-ordinating dimensions of building components, giving first preference to multiples of 300 mm, second preference to multiples of 100 mm and for sizes not greater than 300 mm a third preference to multiples of 50 mm with a fourth preference of 25 mm.

The problems encountered with metrication lie not in the theory or design but in the practicalities of maintenance and adaptation work. At present most of the maintenance and adaptation work is carried out on buildings and structures which were designed and constructed to imperial measures and unfortunately the two systems are not directly compatible.

Many examples can be quoted to show this non-compatibility of imperial and metric components and the following example is given to illustrate the problem:

A window opening is required in a wall to an extension built with standard bricks to accommodate a three-light window. From builders merchants catalogues it has been established that both imperial and metric versions of the proposed window are available and there is no significant difference in price. Should the new window be imperial or metric? The chosen format is a softwood three-light window with two casement sashes and a central top-hung ventlight, the overall dimensions being:

imperial 1809 wide × 1225 high
metric   1800 wide × 1200 high

The number of bricks required to form a suitable opening are:

Imperial – horizontal

$$= \frac{\text{window width}}{\text{brick format size}} \quad = \frac{1809}{225} \quad = 8.04 \text{ bricks}$$

width

$$= \frac{\text{window height}}{\text{brick course height}} \quad = \frac{1225}{76.2} \quad = 16.07 \text{ courses}$$

Metric – horizontal $\quad = \dfrac{1880}{225} \quad = 8 \text{ bricks}$

vertical $\quad = \dfrac{1200}{76.2} \quad = 15.74 \text{ courses}$

It can be seen from the above that in the imperial case with a slight joint adjustment the horizontal dimension can be formed in complete bricks, but with the vertical coursing only the imperial window facilitates complete courses with a slight joint adjustment. The metric window could also have such an adjustment but it would not be in keeping with good bricklaying techniques. The only alternative is to use a stooled lintel forming a dummy joint, or if bricks are to be exposed on the face to use cut bricks over the opening – see Fig. 3.3.

The above conclusion seems obvious since imperial windows are designed to suit imperial brickwork; similarly metric windows are designed to be co-ordinated with metric brickwork – therefore why not use metric brickwork? Metric modular bricks have format sizes of:

200 × 100 × 75; 300 × 100 × 75
200 × 100 × 100; 300 × 100 × 100

These sizes do not dimensionally co-ordinate with imperial window and door sizes as would be expected and neither do they co-ordinate with existing imperial brick coursing which makes junctions between new and existing

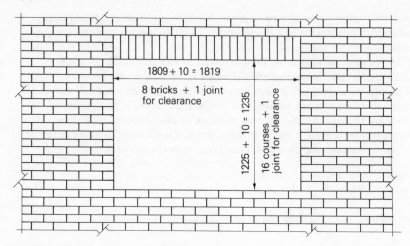

Imperial brickwork opening for imperial window

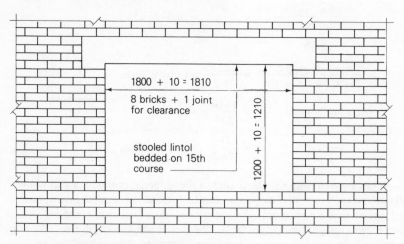

Imperial brickwork opening for metric window

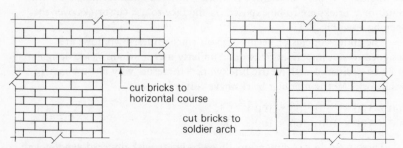

Alternative head treatments for metric window

Fig. 3.3. Example of metrication problems

work difficult to execute in a workmanlike manner; either the joint can be hidden by a rainwater pipe or corner fillet or the difference in bed joint thickness has to be accepted. Another problem is the bonding: traditional brickwork is quarter bonding, whereas metric modular brickwork is third bonding, and also, because of their size, they are heavier and are not popular with bricklayers and this has led to a reduction in output by the brick manufacturers to less than 2 per cent of the total facing brick production.

The same argument can be put forward regarding doors, since metric doors are larger in width and height than their imperial counterparts. In the context of replacement doors and windows, then obviously unless structural alterations are acceptable it is economically better to replace imperial doors and windows with imperial sizes and not to contemplate using metric co-ordinated versions. When considering the replacement of fitments such as basins and water closets, the services connected to these items are relatively flexible and therefore adjustment to a metric fitment is fairly simple, using special adaptors where necessary.

The choice between imperial and metric replacements does present a problem with regard to stock holdings, as whether to hold a stock of both types or to concentrate on one or the other. Several factors would have to be considered:

1. Cost: this must include both capital and fixing costs.

2. Availability: dimensional co-ordination to metric modular sizes is very good in theory, but because of the demand for standard imperial sized components, many manufacturers are producing only a limited range of metric products.

3. Future trends: as metrication and dimensional co-ordination become more acceptable, the current reluctance to change may be reversed and the stock holding policy must therefore be flexible enough to accommodate such trends.

Consideration of the three factors given above should enable an economic policy with regard to stock holding to be formulated. This policy will vary according to the enterprise and as to whether the stock being held is intended primarily for repairs and replacement or for possible adaptation and extension work.

Financial aid

Financial aid in the form of grants is available for certain maintenance, rehabilitation and renovation operations, particularly in connection with housing. Various grants for the improvement and repair of sound older homes (usually considered to be pre-1961) are available under the Housing Act 1974. These grants are provided by local authorities with government assistance.

The Housing Act 1974 was designed to provide the maximum financial assistance to those areas in greatest need and to this end grants are available on three levels depending on the type of area in which the premises are situated. These areas are designated by the local authority with the approval of the Secretary of State and are as follows:

1. Housing Action Areas: these are areas which the local authority consider to be unsatisfactory in terms of living conditions and that such conditions can be most effectively dealt with by improvement within a five-year period. The amount of grant payable is based on the 'eligible expense' and may be up to 75 per cent of this sum or in cases of hardship up to 90 per cent with a maximum grant limit as laid down according to the type of grant being sought.

2. General Improvement Areas: these are areas which do not qualify as housing action areas but still require modernization to bring them up to present-day standards. A general improvement area has to either surround or have a common boundary with a Housing Action Area. The grant is 60 per cent of the 'eligible expense' subject to the maximum amount according to the grant being sought.

3. General Areas: these are areas other than those given above and qualify for a grant of up to 50 per cent of 'eligible expenses' subject to the maximum of the grant being sought.

The conditions and values of the various grants available are set out in the Housing Act 1974 and these can usually be obtained from the local authority in the form of a guide which gives the current values and conditions for the types of grant available. There are basically four types of grant for which application can be made under this Act and these are:

1. Improvement grants: these are made at the discretion of the local authority to help owners improve older houses to an acceptable standard, or to provide dwellings by converting houses of an unsatisfactory size. Generally, grants will not be given for the installation of a central heating system unless it forms part of a more comprehensive scheme of improvement. The main conditions of such a grant are that the dwelling:

(*a*) can be provided with all the standard amenities for the exclusive use of its occupants;
(*b*) will be in good repair;
(*c*) will conform to such structural or other requirements as may be specified by the Secretary of State;
(*d*) will provide satisfactory accommodation for at least thirty years but if the above conditions cannot be met at reasonable expense the period can be reduced to a period of not less than ten years.

2. Intermediate grants: these are made by local authorities to help meet the cost of improving houses by providing any missing amenities where these have not been present for the previous twelve months. Similar conditions as those quoted for improvement grants are imposed except the useful life is reduced to fifteen years.

3. *Special grants:* made at the discretion of local authorities towards the cost of providing standard amenities which will improve a dwelling which provides accommodation for more than one family and are for the exclusive use of the residents in the multiple-occupied dwelling.

4. *Repair grants:* these are available only for dwellings in Housing Action Areas or General Improvement Areas, enabling a dwelling to be brought into good repair (disregarding internal decoration) having regard to its age, character and locality. Such grants are made for works not associated with works of improvement or conversion and are limited to applicants who could not finance the work without undue hardship.

Historic buildings

The Historic Building and Ancient Monument Act 1953 established Historic Buildings Councils to advise the Secretary of State on the allocations of grants for the purpose of defraying in whole or in part any expenditure incurred in the repair or maintenance of a building which is considered to be of outstanding historical or architectural interest, including their contents and adjoining land. Conditions such as access by the public to the whole or part of the property may well be imposed with the issue of such a grant.

Other financial sources

Apart from the grants described above, other sources of finance available are generally in the form of loans on which interest is paid, the principal sources being:

1. *Commercial banks:* subject to some form of satisfactory security or collateral, a loan or overdraft can often be arranged. In the case of a loan, a set sum of money is transferred to the client either in cash or to his account on which an agreed rate of interest is paid until the debt is completely repaid. Overdrafts, however, give permission for the client to overdraw on his account up to an agreed amount, interest being charged only on the amount overdrawn.

2. *Building societies:* these will arrange mortgages for the purchase of land and buildings on a long-term basis with probably the most favourable interest rates of all methods of obtaining finance, but there is a time delay of at least several weeks before the money becomes available whilst the agreement is being drawn up.

3. *Finance companies:* loans from these sources are usually arranged by a merchant or trader from whom the client wishes to purchase some

commodity, but the agreement is between the client and the finance company on what is known as hire purchase.

4. *Insurance companies:* mortgages can be arranged by these companies and this is usually carried out by purchasing an endowment policy. The client usually pays interest only on the mortgage and at maturity the company will be repaid the capital loaned and any accrued profits on the policy being paid to the client.

As with the question of responsibility for repairs and maintenance, it is essential that at the time of preparing an economic feasibility or assessment study the conditions and rates of interest of financing the proposal or project are thoroughly investigated and taken into account to achieve a realistic and economic solution.

Taxation

Works of repair and maintenance are subject to Value Added Tax at the standard rate, whereas alteration works, like those of new works, are zero rated, therefore when assessments are being made an allowance for Value Added Tax must be included to achieve an accurate figure. Consideration must also be given to any tax reductions which may be allowable under various government taxation and grant schemes such as special grants and tax relief available for particular areas where investment and expansion is being encouraged.

The actual conditions under which tax relief and grants can be obtained varies with government policies and is set out in the Finance Acts which should be consulted when making economic appraisals for the maintenance and adaptation of buildings.

Chapter 4

Legislation

The term legislation comes from the Latin *legis*, of law; *latio*, proposing; however, in modern usage it means the making of law. In most countries this is done by an elected body called an assembly, congress or parliament which has taken over the original powers of a sovereign or supreme ruler. The sovereign declares the law but does not create it.

In this country the formation of law is by the Queen in Parliament. In the British system the Cabinet presents a draft Bill in Parliament where it is 'read' for the first time and then printed. The second reading is the occasion for a general debate on the principles embodied in the proposed Bill, if there is a majority vote in favour of the second reading the Bill is then considered by a committee of the whole House, a standing committee or a select committee. Amendments to the original draft are considered at this committee stage and the amended Bill is then 'reported' to the House. At this report stage there may well be further amendments but if there is a majority vote in favour of it the Bill is read a third time. The Bill is then taken to the House of Lords for consideration and when the two Houses have given the Bill their approval it receives the Royal Assent and becomes an Act of Parliament, which is also known as a statute. The procedure for a private member's Bill is similar to that described above for the general law making process.

Acts of Parliament may be passed to alter existing laws or for the purposes of creating new law. Each Parliament is supreme in its own power and can repeal or alter any Act created by its predecessors. The complexity of modern society and the technologies it uses has meant that in modern times Parliament has had to resort frequently to delegated legislation.

Delegated legislation

Delegated legislation is sometimes referred to as secondary law, an Act of Parliament being primary law, and is the handing over of legislative powers to some other body. This is necessary so that those who have detailed knowledge in a particular field can be consulted and can give advice on the precise details to be set out in a delegated legislative document known as a Statutory Instrument. The Minister or Secretary of State to whom the responsibility is delegated is usually too busy or does not have the necessary technical knowledge to write the regulations himself and therefore an advisory committee is set up to formulate the regulations to be contained within the Statutory Instrument. The Minister's function is therefore to sign the document containing the regulations and in so doing gives his and Parliament's authority to it.

So that the supreme power of the Queen in Parliament remains, there are safeguards to the introduction of regulations contained within a Statutory Instrument. The doctrine of *ultra vires* (beyond the powers of) can be applied, which means that delegated legislation can be challenged in the courts on the grounds that the party to whom the power was delegated has acted beyond the power granted to him. Under the Statutory Instruments Act 1949 the proposed Statutory Instrument may be submitted to Parliament and will cease to be operative if either House so decides within forty days. The Act under which the power was delegated determines whether the Statutory Instrument must be laid before Parliament and whether it needs the approval of both Houses. Local authority byelaws is another example of delegated legislation which may have to be approved or confirmed by a Minister or Secretary of State before it can be enacted. As with Statutory Instruments, delegated legislation conferred in a local authority is subject to the doctrine of *ultra vires*.

Acts of Parliament can create private duties only or they can create statutory provisions to be carried out by the public sector. Most Acts which create private duties are concerned with duty of care and have been passed to overcome some of the problems encountered when applying common law principles. Common law in its earliest form consisted of customs and usages but it is now based on the principles set out by generations of judges trying the cases before them, thus creating precedents. From the numerous judgments given on any particular subject the lawyer must try to deduce a principle which will help him to solve any problem which may arise. Common law is therefore a building up of case law which generally owes its origin to ancient custom and is therefore unwritten law. Two Acts of Parliament which created private duties, in terms of buildings, are the Defective Premises Act 1972 and the Occupiers' Liability Act 1957.

Defective Premises Act 1972

This Act came into existence as a direct result of the Law Commission No. 40 Report. The Law Commission is a body of lawyers whose task is to examine different branches of law and to report with a view to reform and is a result of the Law Commission Act 1965. Their concern in this instance was the common law principle of *caveat emptor* (let the buyer beware) which means that the buyer would have to accept the building as he found it unless there was a condition to the contrary in his contract of purchase. In the case of house purchases the Law Commission felt that this was unreasonable since to establish that the dwelling was not defective in any way would mean that a costly survey of the premises would be necessary. Purchasers of industrial and commercial properties however, did not need legal protection since adequate professional advice as to the condition and suitability of the premises was usually sought before the signing of contracts.

Notwithstanding the fact that many new dwellings came under the National House Building Council's protection scheme, the Law Commission felt that the scheme did not provide a remedy in all cases, such as dwellings built outside the scheme, conversions and extensions, therefore there was a need to amend the law as to liability for injury or damages caused to persons through defects in the state of the premises.

The Act imposes a duty to build dwellings properly, that is in a workmanlike or professional manner with proper materials and that the dwelling be fit for habitation when completed. This duty is owed to the person who purchases the house or who pays for the work of conversion or extension and also extends to others who acquire the house from the initial purchaser or the person who paid for the works originally. This duty is therefore imposed upon builders, subcontractors, architects, designers and surveyors who take on this type of work and since this is a statutory duty it cannot be excluded by any terms set out in a contract. Local authorities and others who arrange for a contractor to carry out the work, such as developers, are also included in those who owe this duty set out in the Act. In respect of a claim under the Act it would be for the courts to decide, each case being considered on its own merit.

If a builder carries out the work in accordance with the plans and specifications given to him by the client's architect or designer, he is not liable if his work does not result in a dwelling fit for habitation, since his compliance with the plans and specification discharges his obligations under the Act unless he is subject to any duty to warn a person of any defect in the instructions; this would occur if he was taking direct instructions from his client who does not have the technical knowledge to issue such instructions.

If a person wishes to make a claim for breach of duty he must bring such a claim under the Act within six years starting from the day the dwelling was completed; however, a claim under common law for the tort of negligence can be made within six years of the discovery of the defective work. This six-year rule also applies to any remedial work carried out to rectify a fault. Therefore if a builder carries out remedial work three years after completion he remains liable for the remedial work for the next six years.

A landlord whose agreement with his tenant requires him to maintain and repair the premises also has a duty of care to all persons who might reasonably be expected to be affected by defects in the state of the premises. He must take reasonable care to see that such persons are safe from personal injury and that their property is safe from damage caused by a defect in the premises.

In common with most Acts of Parliament the Act does not work in retrospect and therefore only applies to premises which were completed, let or disposed of in any way on or after the Act came into force on 1 January 1974.

Occupiers' Liability Act 1957

This Act was passed to try to clarify the duty of care owed by an occupier to those who come on to his land. Under common law persons who entered on to another's land were classed as invitees, licensees or trespassers. A duty of care was owed to the invitees and licensees but not to a trespasser, since he took the land as he found it and therefore if he suffered an injury as a result of being on the land he had no claim against the occupier.

The courts when reaching their decision would often, in the case of children, find reasons why the child was not a trespasser but an invitee or licensee, so that an award of damages could be made. The Occupiers' Liability Act 1957 made one class of person to whom a duty of care was owed, that of a lawful visitor, but it did not change the law regarding trespassers. Therefore persons who enter another's land to do business, such as firms' representatives, would be clients and persons entering the land because of their calling such as postmen are owed a duty of care even though they do not have the occupier's written or oral consent.

Trespassers, however, have no such duty owed to them, but the occupier may only take reasonable steps to remove them from his land. What is reasonable in any particular circumstance is for the courts to decide. The exception to this general rule is in the case of children, which is legally anyone under the age of eighteen, but age is taken into account. A youth of seventeen would not be treated in the same manner as, say, a child of four or five, and if the court was satisfied that the child had the maturity and understanding to appreciate the dangers on the land he would be treated as an adult trespasser.

It must be remembered that a building site contains many allurements to children in the form of ladders, machinery, stacks of bricks and fires for burning rubbish and that this attraction is there all the time and not just during working hours. The position of the occupier in his liability towards child trespassers was reviewed by the House of Lords in the case of *British Railways Board* v *Herrington* 1972.

Herrington was a six-year-old boy who was playing with his two brothers in a public field next to an electrified line owned by the British Railways Board. A chain link fence guarding the track was damaged at a point where the footpath went alongside the track to a footbridge. Employees of the British Railways Board had reported that children were using the broken fence to gain access to their land, and were taking a short cut across the tracks. No action was taken by the Board. Herrington went through the gap in the fence and walked along the track where he was severely injured by the electric line. He sued for damages. The British Railways Board argued that he was a trespasser since the electric line did not constitute an allurement and therefore no duty of care was owed. The House of Lords decided that the British Railways Board was liable since it had allowed the fence to remain in a damaged condition and this had allowed the child to go on to the line where there was serious danger in the form of an electric line with which the child had come into contact. Lord Reid in making his judgment considered the standard of care which can be expected from the occupier is dependent on his knowledge, ability and resources.

Another case which highlights the duty of care owed by an occupier in the context of children under this Act is that of *Pannet* v *P. McGuiness and Company* (1972). The latter were demolition contractors who lit fires inside a derelict warehouse they were demolishing to burn off the rubbish. The warehouse was next to a public park used by children. Three men were appointed to feed the fires, keep them under control and to look out for and warn off children. James Pannet, a five-year-old boy, had been told by his mother to keep away from the warehouse but he had entered the warehouse after school, fell into a fire and was burned. Children had been chased away by the contractor's men but they had returned. The contractor contended that the child was a trespasser and that they had done all that was required of them by law. In the Court of Appeal Lord Denning said that although the contractor had chased children away this was before any fires were lighted. These created an extra hazard and called for the contractor to take extra steps in keeping a good look-out so as to keep out trespassing children. They had failed to do this so the contractor was liable for the damages suffered by James Pannet.

In arriving at his conclusion Lord Denning made the following points which are worthy of note:

1. You must apply common sense.
2. You must take into account also the character of the intrusion by the trespasser.
3. You must also have regard to the nature of the place where the trespass occurs.
4. You must also take into account the knowledge the defendant has, or ought to have, of the likelihood of trespassers being present.

From the above examples it is clear that contractors, whether engaged in new or maintenance work, are vulnerable in the matter of occupiers' liability by the very nature of the work they carry out and this is especially true where children are concerned.

Acts of Parliament relating to building standards

The principal Acts of Parliament relating to building standards are generally concerned with matters of health and safety which are embodied in the Act itself, whereas the detailed requirements are set out in the form of regulations contained in Statutory Instruments. The principal Acts controlling building standards are:

Public Health Acts 1936 and 1961

Legislators have over the centuries tried to control building activities in the context of health and safety, such as the London Building Act 1667 which was introduced after the Great Fire in 1666. Insanitary conditions, particularly during the industrial revolution, led to a series of Public Health Acts which gave power to local health boards to make byelaws to control certain standards of new construction; however, these byelaws were only local and not national.

The Public Health Act 1936 transferred this power to local authorities who made their own byelaws or had to adopt Model Building Byelaws which enabled them to control the safety and health aspects of new buildings, a great emphasis being placed on the problems of sanitation and drainage. The Public Health Act 1961 made provision for the introduction of national regulations to control all forms of building construction. The first regulations of this kind appeared in 1965 and applied to England and Wales with the exception of London, who had their own stringent regulations. Scotland, because of its different legal system, has its own building regulations.

These regulations were issued in the form of a Statutory Instrument and its enforcement was left in the hands of the local authorities through their building control officers. Since their first introduction there have been many amendments and in 1972 the Building Regulations were reissued to consolidate the amendments and to allow for the regulations to be metricated and this was followed by a further consolidation and reissue in 1976.

In the context of maintenance the Building Regulations have only a limited control and this is mainly concerned with the fitness of materials which is contained in Part B. However, if the maintenance entails structural alteration, extension works and/or change of use the full regulations apply. Under Section 65 of the Public Health Act 1961 the local authority can require the removal of or alterations to any work which does not comply with the regulations or which was undertaken without proper approval. Under the 1961 Act the local authority is allowed to withdraw its approval if the work has not been commenced within three years of obtaining Building Regulation approval. The Act also requires that notice shall be given to the local authority for the demolition of buildings.

Housing Acts 1957 and 1969

These Acts laid down the standards for residential premises in terms of fabric condition, services and equipment, internal layout and the quality of the surrounding environment. Minimum standards below which the premises could be adjudged unfit for human habitation are set out in Section 4 of the Housing Act 1957 and this basically covers any aspect of the building which may pose a threat to health or safety of the occupants such as the state of repair, stability, dampness, ventilation, water supply and drainage.

The Housing Act 1969 in Section 72 gives the local authority power to take action before a house actually becomes unfit. They can serve notice upon the person who has control of the premises to carry out necessary repairs and maintenance if they are satisfied that such substantial repairs are needed to bring the house up to a reasonable standard, having regard to its age, character and locality. What is a satisfactory standard is debatable but generally local authorities base their decision on guidance circulars sent out by the appropriate government department.

Town and Country Planning Act 1971

This Act gave authority for planning to be vested in local authorities who are charged with the responsibility of surveying their area and producing plans of how they proposed that the area should be developed and used in the future. All aspects of planning including such things as conservation, social considerations, economic, environmental and physical condition must be taken into account.

These plans take one of two forms:

1. *Structure plan:* this consists of a written statement of the local authority's intentions for the area for the next twenty years. It has to be submitted to the Secretary of State for approval after the plan has had adequate publicity so that representations can be made to the local authority by those likely to be affected by it. Any subsequent changes to the approved structure plan must also be submitted for approval and any areas which are to be extensively developed must be begun within ten years of the approval being granted. These areas are known as action areas.

2. *Local plans:* these are elaborations of the action areas shown on structure plans and consist of written details with a map. They do not require the approval of the Secretary of State but as with structure plans they must be published to allow for public participation and representation by those likely to be affected by such a plan.

These plans enable the local authority to control development within their area by using this as a basis for the issue of development certificates and permits. In the case of industrial developments a certificate is required from the Department of Trade and Industry for the following situations:

1. Any new industrial development.
2. Extension to an existing building which will exceed 464 m^2.
3. Change of use from non-industrial to industrial usage.

Office development permits may be required from the Department of the Environment especially if the proposed development exceeds 929 m^2. These permits have been introduced to control office developments in and around the congested area of London. These permits apply to extensions and changes of usage as well as to new developments.

When making application for planning permission under the Town and Country Planning Act 1971 and as amended in 1972 a certificate of ownership is necessary according to the type of ownership held. Application is made either for outline or detailed planning permission:

1. *Outline planning permission:* the application consists of a plan of the land layout and drawings of the type of development proposed to enable the authority to check if it is in accordance with the structure and local plans. Approval is granted for three years by the end of which a detailed planning application must be made.

2. *Detailed planning permission:* this form of application consists of suitable plans, drawings and specification of the proposed development. If approved, the work has to be commenced within five years or a fresh application has to be made.

Planning permission does not give automatic Building Regulation approval since they are based on different considerations, therefore after obtaining planning permission Building Regulation approval must be sought.

Certain alterations can be made to a house without obtaining planning permission and these are known as permitted developments; some of these permitted alterations are shown in a simplified and diagrammatical form in Fig. 4.1. As with planning permissions, permitted developments do not give automatic exemption from Building Regulation approval which must be obtained from the local authority in the usual manner.

Fire Precautions Act 1971

The purpose of this Act is to make certain public and residential buildings safer in the event of a fire. It does not include buildings already covered by other statutory provisions such as offices, shops and factories. It is one of the few Acts relative to buildings which can be operated in retrospect by ordering existing premises to be upgraded to present day requirements and standards.

Premises are brought under the Act by the issue of a designating order by the Secretary of State which makes regulations appertaining to that type or class of building. The occupier must obtain a fire certificate showing compliance with the regulations from the fire authority within a specified time or before the premises can be used for the intended purpose. The basic requirements are usually:

1. Adequate means of escape.
2. Unobstructed and clearly marked escape routes and exits.
3. Adequate fire alarm system.
4. Staff to be trained in fire drill.

The certificate may also impose requirements relating to the maintenance of escape routes and other fire precautions specified in the certificate.

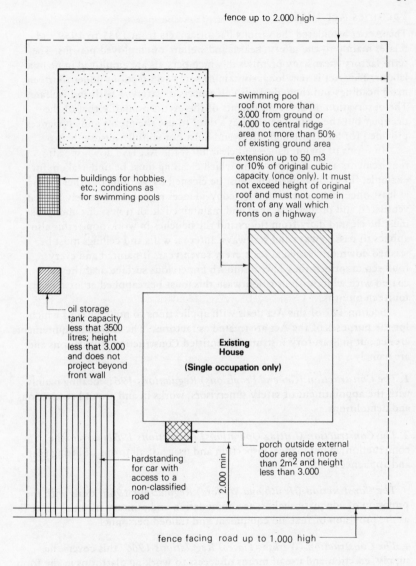

fence up to 2.000 high

swimming pool
roof not more
than 3.000 from ground or
4.000 to central ridge
area not more than 50%
of existing ground area

buildings for hobbies,
etc.; conditions as
for swimming pools

extension up to 50 m3
or 10% of original cubic
capacity (once only). It must
not exceed height of original
roof and must not come in
front of any wall which
fronts on a highway

oil storage
tank capacity
less that 3500
litres; height
less that 3.000
and does not
project beyond
front wall

**Existing
House**

(Single occupation only)

hardstanding
for car with
access to a
non-classified
road

2.000 min

porch outside external
door area not more
than 2m² and height
less than 3.000

fence facing road up to 1.000 high

No change in external appearance is permitted without
planning permission except for repairs and decorations.

Fig. 4.1. Permitted development for houses

Factories Act 1961

This Act consolidated the various Factories Acts from 1937 to 1959 and relates mainly to the safety, health and welfare of employed persons. The term factory means any premises in which persons are employed in manual labour. This Act is very long, containing some 185 sections under fourteen main headings and these deal with all aspects of safety, health and welfare. The observation of the requirements of this Act is primarily that of the occupier but the employee also has a duty to use the means and appliances provided for his health and safety and must not wilfully misuse them.

In terms of maintenance and cleanliness the Act lays down specific requirements as to periods within which cleaning must be undertaken; for example, floors of workrooms must be cleaned by washing or other means at least once every week, sanitary conveniences must be adequately lighted, ventilated and properly cleaned and maintained at all times, dirt and refuse must be cleared daily from floors and the benches in workrooms; this also applies to passageways and stairways. Internal walls and ceilings must be washed down or cleaned at least every seven years if painted and every fourteen months if they have a smooth impervious surface or if they are coated with whitewash or colourwash this must be reapplied at least every fourteen months.

Section 127 of this Act deals with applications to building sites which for the purposes of the Act are treated as factories. The detailed requirements are set out in Statutory Instruments entitled Construction Regulations and are namely:

1. *The Construction (General Provisions) Regulations 1961:* dealing mainly with the appointment of safety supervisors, works in and around excavations and demolitions.

2. *The Construction (Lifting Operations) Regulations 1961:* covers the construction, maintenance, inspection and usage of all forms of lifting gear and appliances.

3. *The Construction (Health and Welfare) Regulations 1966:* deals with the provision of adequate shelter, accommodation and sanitary facilities as well as the provision of first aid equipment and trained personnel.

4. *The Construction (Working Places) Regulations 1966:* this covers the supply, erection and use of means of access to working platforms in the form of trestles, scaffolds and gantries.

Offices, Shops and Railway Premises Act 1963

This Act has similar intentions to that of the Factories Act quoted above but covers employees in offices, shops and buildings occupied by railway under-takers in the immediate vicinity of the permanent way. The main duty falls on the occupier to observe the requirements of the Act which covers such items as cleaning requirements (no dirt or refuse must be allowed to accumulate, premises to be kept clean and floors to be washed or swept at least once a week), overcrowding, minimum temperatures, ventilation, lighting, sanitary facilities, means of escape in case of fire and general fire precautions. All of these aspects must be maintained to at least the minimum requirements and standards imposed by this Act.

Health and Safety at Work, etc., Act 1974

The purpose of this Act is to provide the legislative framework to promote, stimulate and encourage high standards of health and safety at work. It is an enabling Act in addition to and only partially replacing existing health and safety at work legislation such as those described above for factories and offices. The greater part of the existing Acts and subsidiary regulations remain current but repeal, amendment, revision and updating will continue as necessary over the coming years.

The Act is in three parts, the first two dealing with matters of health and safety administered by the Department of Employment and the third part deals with the Building Regulations administered by the Department of the Environment. The Act itself does not create or amend new or existing regulations but it does extend the scope of subjects upon which regulations may be made and to increase the flexibility of procedures for building control. The first amendment to the Building Regulations 1976 made under this Act came into operation on 1 June 1979 in the form of a Statutory Instrument making regulations for the conservation of fuel and power in buildings other than dwellings. This is a good example of the extended scope of subjects since under the Public Health Acts, because of the doctrine of *ultra vires*, regulations for fuel conservation could not have been made.

If a member of Her Majesty's Factory Inspectorate discovers a contravention of one of the provisions of the existing Acts or regulations or a contravention of a provision of the new Act he can:

1. Issue a prohibition notice: this is used if there is a risk of serious injury, to stop the activity giving rise to this risk, until the remedial action specified in the notice has been taken. The notice can be served on the person undertaking the activity or on the person in control of it. The notice can take effect immediately it is served or at a later date and such a notice can be issued whether or not there has been a legal contravention.

2. Issue an improvement notice: this is used where there is a legal contravention of any of the statutory regulations, to remedy the fault within a specified time limit. As with the previous notice, it can be served on the person deemed to be contravening a statutory regulation or on any person on whom responsibilities are placed.

3. Prosecute: any person contravening a relevant statutory provision instead of or in addition to serving one of the above notices or any person who fails to comply with a notice served upon him. Contravention can lead to prosecution summarily in a Magistrates' Court or Sheriff's Court in Scotland or an indictment in the Crown Courts of England and Wales or the Sheriff's Court in Scotland depending on the regulation which has been contravened. Fines on summary conviction can be up to £400 whereas there is no limit to the fine which can be imposed on conviction on indictment. Certain offences can result in imprisonment for up to two years.

Any person on whom a notice has been served has the right of appeal to an industrial tribunal against the notice itself or any of the conditions or terms contained within the notice.

4. *Seize, render harmless or destroy:* this can be carried out by an inspector if he considers any substance or article to be the cause of imminent danger or serious personal injury.

Dangerous or dilapidated buildings

Section 58 of the Public Health Act 1936, as amended by the Public Health Act 1961, provides that if it appears to a local authority that any building or structure or part of the same is in a dangerous condition or is used to carry such loads as to be dangerous, the local authority may apply to a court of summary jurisdiction for an order requiring the owner of the building to carry out such work as may be necessary or to demolish the structure and remove any rubbish. If the danger arises from overloading, the court may make an order restricting the use of the building until it is satisfied that any necessary works have been executed.

Section 24 of the Public Health Act 1961 extends these provisions to buildings which are dangerous to persons in the street and Section 25 gives a local authority the power to carry out emergency measures if it considers that such steps are necessary to overcome the danger. Also under this Act a local authority can, after serving notice, carry out any necessary works where any premises are in a defective state so as to be prejudicial to health or a nuisance, and if the building or structure is considered to be detrimental to the amenities of the neighbourhood. The owner can by serving notice within seven days undertake to carry out the necessary work himself. Neglected sites and dilapidated buildings can be dealt with in a similar manner by the local authority requiring the owner to repair or demolish the building or structure and to clear away the rubbish.

It can be seen from the above-mentioned forms of legislation that a great deal of control through Acts of Parliament and Statutory Instruments can be exercised over the construction, repair, maintenance and adaptation of buildings, therefore a good working knowledge of the responsibilities of owners, occupiers and individuals is necessary when consideration is being given to any of these activities. A great deal of control is also given to local authorities who should be consulted as to the precise requirements with regard to planning, Building Regulations and duties owed if any doubt whatsoever exists.

Chapter 5

Deterioration and defects

It is an accepted fact that all materials deteriorate either by age, the action of other forces such as the weather, poor selection of materials which are in contact with one another and react in a deleterious manner, the human factors of ignorance and vandalism, and biological agencies such as insect and fungi attack. If we are to be successful in our design and maintenance policies for buildings it is essential that we understand the principal ways in which deterioration occurs so that we can design against it, recognize it and take the necessary remedial measures in good time. In design terms it is important that the selection and detail of materials and components is made to lessen the effects of deterioration and so increase their durability. Durability is the rate at which deterioration occurs and is usually quoted in terms of the minimum number of years of satisfactory service. Satisfactory service can of course be subjective since an applied finish such as paint which is no longer visually acceptable is only a deterioration in appearance as opposed to a deterioration in the composition of the material or the component to which the paint was applied. The topic of deterioration was considered briefly in Chapter 1 when considering basic principles and this chapter intends to expand on some of the comments made in Chapter 1.

Human factors

The effects of deterioration can be minimized, slowed down or abated by taking the correct action at the appropriate time. Unfortunately many people do not know when is the appropriate time or what is the correct action to take and therefore the deterioration accelerates. As described in the chapter on design considerations, there is a large number of sources of information available to aid the uninformed as to suitable remedial measures and some of these will be considered in the next chapter dealing with the causes and methods of repair. Knowing what, when, where and how to carry out these measures does not ensure that they are in fact undertaken. This is very often caused by not knowing where the true responsibility lies for repairs and maintenance and therefore a working knowledge of the legal aspects is required. Failure to provide the necessary capital either by poor budgeting or poor allocation of financial resources may be at fault. Delay in attending to the problem by a lackadaisical attitude to maintenance can also heighten the problem of deterioration, as can the use of cheaper or unsuitable materials with the misconception that it is economic to maintain buildings cheaply and often rather than use more expensive materials and skilled labour for a long-term treatment. All these aspects tend to add to the deterioration of materials and components but do not necessarily cause it; this can very often be attributed to the selection and/or use of the materials at the initial stages of design and construction.

A simple illustration of this is the common use of ferrous metal fixings in conjunction with an unsuitable material such as oak, which contains gallic acid which will corrode ferrous metals. The use of unsuitable materials in juxtaposition can result in corrosion, unsightly staining and even to the breakdown of some components. It may well be that the choice of materials and design details were prepared in good faith and that the designer did not know or realize the result of his actions, but with the emphasis now being placed on feedback information and the publication of such information the question which must be asked is: Did the designer check with available data before specifying or detailing?

The operative on site can be just as guilty of promoting unnecessary deterioration within buildings by substituting materials, components or fixings where there is a delay or shortage of those specified without first consulting the designer as to their suitability and acceptance; this is particularly true where hidden work is concerned. It can be seen therefore that human error due to ignorance of the consequences of an action can promote and accelerate the deterioration of buildings but this action can also be deliberate in the form of vandalism.

Vandalism is very difficult to overcome and design against. It is not something which is new; indeed, the original vandals were an ancient Germanic people who invaded Western Europe in the fourth and fifth centuries, leaving in their wake a trail of destruction; but the present high level of vandalism in this country probably has its roots in social considerations. The Building Research Establishment conducted a study into vandalism in the context of housing estates (BRE Digest 132) which makes recommendations of methods to discourage and reduce the amount of wilful damage which can be done by vandals and emphasizes the need to set an example by good maintenance, since it has been shown that buildings and site works in a dilapidated state breed vandalism.

Chemical factors

One of the major tasks of maintenance is cleaning, and to lessen the burdens of both time and cost it is an aspect which the designer must consider very carefully by posing the questions: How easy is it to clean? How quickly will it become dirty and how can it be cleaned? The latter question needs very careful consideration since some cleaning operations or methods can increase the deterioration of the materials. Floors can be designed to be polished or washed or cleaned and maintained by a combination of both methods. Polished floors are generally easier to maintain and clean and have good wearing properties but they can become slippery and dangerous if over-polished. Some polishes can have a detrimental affect on the material; for example, an asphalt floor finish will soften unless an emulsion polish is used. Timber floor finishes can swell and warp if over-watered during washing; therefore, the specifier must take care in his selection of materials since it cannot be guaranteed that the user will follow the correct procedure and use the appropriate cleaning agents.

By far the greatest chemical factor, in the context of deterioration, is that of corrosion which is a local destruction of a metal, as in the rusting of ferrous metals such as iron and steel by either chemical or electro-chemical agencies. Corrosion is a result of the instability of metals which therefore tend to reach a more stable state by combining with the surrounding elements such as air, water, soil, sulphur and carbon dioxide. Atmospheric corrosion means oxidation of the metal to form an oxide mixed with hydrated carbonates which leaves a surface film on the metal which, in the case of non-ferrous metals, is a protective.

Most types of water that come into contact with metals can cause dissolution – albeit slight – but this can cause dissolved particles of dissimilar metals to come into contact, which may cause corrosion by an electro-chemical process. The two main governing factors as to the rate of corrosion are the acidity and temperature of the water: the greater the acid level and the higher the temperature the greater will be the corrosive effect. If unfamiliar with the district the advice of the local water authority should always be sought to ascertain the best metal to use for water services in that particular area.

Corrosion may take several forms:

1. Local corrosion: usually called pitting of the surface. The corrosion is limited to the pitted area; the surfaces between the pits being more or less unaffected or stable.

2. General corrosion: here the whole surface is attacked, such as that of an aluminium alloy in contact with strong acids or alkalis.

3. Electrolytic corrosion: sometimes referred to as electro-chemical corrosion and is the result of contact between two dissimilar metals or between a metal and a non-metal, the second material being more electro positive than the material affected. Moisture needs to be present for this form of attack where the potential difference between the metals sets up a galvanic action.

To overcome the problems of corrosion it must be first appreciated that there is a risk of corrosion and how that corrosion will take place. If the source is atmospheric then some form of protective coating should be employed to a corrosive-free base; if the source is electrolytic then isolation is the remedy and this can be achieved by placing a suitable and durable insulator between the two materials.

Furring

One of the problems of deterioration in hot water services within buildings is that of furring, which is a deposit of mineral scale in vessels or pipes in which lime and magnesium-bearing water is heated or conveyed. The degree of furring will depend on the amount of temporary hardness in the water which is caused by the water taking in solution carbonate of calcium or magnesium, depending upon the amount of carbon dioxide in the water, as it passes through the permeable strata of the subsoil. This carbonate becomes bicarbonate as it is dissolved, due to the presence of carbon dioxide, and can be removed by boiling the water.

In the absence of evaporation the fur or scale which is precipitated at temperatures above $60^\circ C$ adheres to the wall of the vessel or pipes. The fur may vary between the extremes of a firmly adhering flint-hard crystalline scale to a soft sand-like scale. In the context of services this furring is undesirable for two reasons:

1. Fur or scale is a poor conductor of heat and therefore serves as an insulator and impedes the transmission of heat from the burner in a boiler to the water.
2. A continual deposit of scale to the bore of a tube or pipe will diminish its bore diameter and hence its flow properties from those used in design calculations and so the system gradually becomes less and less efficient.

To overcome the problems caused by the hardness of water the designer can use a closed system such as the indirect hot water service, or alternatively the water can be treated before use by softening the water by a base exchange or lime soda process. An initially cheaper but not such an efficient or economic method in the long term is to use a direct hot water system with oversized diameter pipes on the primary circuit.

Atmospheric factors

Atmospheric factors are generally referred to as weathering, which is the action of the external climate on exposed materials and components. The reaction and hence the durability of any one particular material to weathering will vary with its physical and chemical properties as well as the function it is expected to perform and also its position and orientation within the structure. Weathering can be defined as a process of decomposition or deterioration caused by the components of the weather such as radiation from the sun, rain, snow, hail, wind, gases and contaminates such as dirt, soot and salt spray. It should also be noted that the external climate can affect the internal environment or climate of a building.

Records, forecasts and climatological studies are undertaken by the Meteorological Office and are available to designers on payment of a nominal fee for the type of service required. The climate is the average condition of the atmosphere for a particular locality or area whereas climatology is the science dealing with climates. The climate is determined by the daily weather events and by overall seasonal patterns which include temperature, humidity, sunshine hours, wind speed and direction, rainfall, amount of cloud and other weather phenomena such as fog and frost.

The natural external environment can be both a hindrance and help to the designer since he is seeking to both invite its aid in his overall design concept and repel its detrimental effects. To make a building habitable and comfortable the designer must seek to control the effects of heat, cold, light, air, moisture and dryness and try to foresee any destructive aspects of the climate. The designer can be aided in the practical aspects of design by climatic or weather trends but he also has to take into account his design in terms of architectural expression and aesthetics; the two may unfortunately conflict with one another. Since this part of the text is considering climate and weathering conditions and not aesthetics it is therefore intended to concentrate solely on the practical aspects of planning.

The orientation or arrangement of the axis of a building is a method of controlling the effects of the sun, wind and rain since the sun is regular in its path and favours the southern aspect of buildings in the northern hemisphere. The building may be orientated to capture the heat of the sun or conversely it may be turned to evade the solar heat for coolness with its thermal expansion problems. Orientation may also be used to control air flow circulation and reduce the disadvantages of wind, rain and snow since in most areas the prevailing currents are predictable. It can therefore be seen that the orientation of a building can help control the local environment but other factors must also be taken into account. The character of the local terrain may have some influence on the final orientation of the building by the way in which undulating ground, trees and adjacent buildings create shade and reduce or intensify the effects of the wind by creating eddies and funnel wind flow patterns. The presence of bodies of water in the form of rivers, lakes and ponds will produce moisture and reflect the sun.

The effects of all these natural forces associated with climate may be modified by design details such as overhanging eaves and porches to produce areas of shade and protection from the rain, roofs pitched to the correct angle for the chosen finish or covering to adequately shed the rain, and the use of screen walling around buildings to reduce or limit the amount of wind, light and heat reaching the external fabric. Colour also plays an important part in the environmental planning aspect of design since apart from its expressive quality there is the practical function of reflecting or absorbing solar rays, since light colours reflect heat and dark colours absorb it.

It must also be remembered that the designer must take into account the climate when planning or trying to create the internal environment of his building. The principal means of controlling this internal environment is the windows or fenestration, since this will control the natural daylight within the building in terms of amount, distribution, intensity, direction and quality by selecting the size, shape, position, texture, transparency and colour of the glazing. Other factors such as ventilation and heating must also be taken into account since most translucent materials conduct heat more readily than their surrounding walls. The use of windows should therefore be limited in extreme climates. Consideration must also be given to the fact that a window is the view out or the means of visual communication from within the building to the outside world and this important function must not be over-ruled by purely practical solutions. Colour and texture can also be used as a controlling medium within the building as well as in external considerations, all of which leads the designer to choosing his materials and formulating details.

The choice of materials will be governed mainly by the following factors:

1. Their own ability to withstand the effects of the climate.
2. Their own ability to fulfil their design function.
3. Their reaction with surrounding materials.
4. Their ease of maintenance and/or replacement.
5. Overall economic acceptability.

The designer's task is to find a successful solution to the above factors by finding and using materials which have acceptable physical and economic advantages over other materials considered. To carry out this analysis the designer must know how the various materials will weather and react with one another. It would be impossible in a text of this nature to consider all the materials and combinations available for incorporation into a building; it is therefore proposed that only the reaction to weathering of the major materials used in building works will be considered under this heading.

Bricks and clay products

Clay products which can be used on the external surfaces include roofing tiles, copings, quarry tiles in flat roof and balcony applications and, of course, bricks. Generally all bricks and clay products have good durability, hence their popularity, since the most common effect of weathering on these products is a change of appearance. Usually they take on a mellow look which is considered to be aesthetically pleasing; however, deterioration in clay products can be caused by frost and the crystallization of soluble salts.

Most bricks and clay products have the ability to absorb moisture, and since our winters are invariably wet and cold the water which can be held in the pores of the material, particularly those near to the exposed surface, can become frozen into ice. This ice formation is accompanied by expansion which can result in flaking or spalling over the surface of the brick or tile; this process can be progressive, gradually reducing the overall thickness of the clay unit. Clay products which are to be situated in an exposed condition should therefore be carefully selected, choosing, in the case of bricks, the dense Class 'A' bricks as defined in BS 3921 for situations such as parapets, retaining and boundary walls.

The most common form of crystallization of soluble salts in the context of clay products and in particular brickwork is efflorescence, which is a white surface deposit of salts in the form of a loose powder or feathery crystals. Generally speaking this form of surface salt deposit is not harmful to the brickwork but it can be disfiguring. It usually occurs when dry weather follows wet weather, as in the spring, and can often be removed by brushing with a stiff brush or being naturally washed away by the rain. Unfortunately there is no really accurate method of predicting or preventing an outbreak of efflorescence which can occur many times before all the salts inherent in the bricks have been removed. In some instances there may be staining which appears to be efflorescence and is difficult to remove and is not washed away by the rain; this is usually due to the action of lime leached from the mortar between the bricks or from adjacent materials such as concrete or limestone copings and sills. If the soluble salts crystallize inside the body of the brickwork instead of on the face, the expansion can cause spalling of the external face, or if the crystallization is near the inner surface the plaster finish could be pushed away from the backing surface.

Moisture movement in clay products is unavoidable but most of the major movement seems to occur when the products are fresh from the kiln and therefore occurs during the normal storage periods before the product is actually incorporated in the building and can therefore for all practical purposes be ignored. This is, however, not true of thermal movements, which can occur quite rapidly during the day; in the summer they can have a temperature change of $11°C$ which can give rise to a 2.5 mm increase in length over a 30-metre run of wall. It is therefore recommended that a 10 mm wide expansion joint should be incorporated every 12 metres in long unrestrained walls.

Very often brick walls deteriorate not because of defects within the bricks or poor selection of materials but because of a deterioration of the mortar bonding the bricks together. This fault, along with others such as defective damp-proof courses, will be considered in the next chapter on causes and methods of repair.

Timber and timber products

Timber is a term used for wood of sufficient size for commercial purposes and is a natural material, each piece having its own characteristics, but within its own species its properties can be defined, an allowance having been made for individual variances. Trees which produce suitable timbers belong to one of two classifications:

1. *Conifers:* these yield the so-called softwoods and this includes the pines, spruces and larches which usually have more or less needle-like leaves.

2. *Deciduous:* these broad-leaf trees yield the hardwoods such as oak, ash, beech and teak.

To appreciate timber as a material its origin and structure must be known. The part of a tree visible above the ground consists of the main trunk and the branch system whose finest branches are the leaf-bearing twigs. The trunk and branches grow in length solely at the tips and grow in diameter by the addition of new wood and bark by microscopically thin layers of cells called the cambium which lies between the inner wood and the bark. The cambium deposits new wood on the outer side of the existing wood and new bark on the inner side of the existing bark, thus pushing the bark outwards. This action produces the characteristic annual rings of timber which increase with breadth until the tree reaches maturity and then diminishes.

The two main components of timber are cellulose, which gives the material its strength and elasticity, and lignin, which is the binding matrix holding the fibres of the material together; but it is the microscopic structure of wood which determines its properties. The cell structure of softwoods is relatively simple, consisting mainly of very narrow, hollow, spindle-shaped fibres called tracheids which run parallel to the long axis of the trunk or branch. Hardwoods have a similar type of cell but it is shorter with a thicker cell wall. This cell structure of timber produces a material which is strong in tension and reasonably strong in compression with good elastic properties and is easy to cut and work. Being a natural material it can, however, have the following natural defects:

1. *Knots:* these are formed by the ends of branches passing through the body of the timber and although forming a feature on the surface they can prove to be a problem. Knots are heavier and denser than the surrounding wood and if they dry out rapidly they can become loose and fall out, leaving a hole or cavity. Knots on the edge of timber are very prone to this fault. Groups of knots or large numbers of knots in any one piece can reduce considerably the general properties associated with that species.

2. *Shakes:* these are splits or crevices caused by unequal shrinkage during seasoning or during growth. Shakes can cause weaknesses in the timber or will entail wastage during working up. They can be of several forms such as heart shakes which radiate from the centre of the piece, being wider at the pith end than at the cambium layer; star shakes also radiate from the centre but are wider at the cambium layer; cup shakes are curved and separate the layers of timber, and thunder shakes, which are clefts running in an irregular zigzag fashion across the grain.

3. *Wany edges:* these occur where the original rounded surface of the tree remains on the edge due to too much sapwood being left in during conversion. A large amount of wane reduces the strength and adds to the difficulty of obtaining an acceptable finish.

In well seasoned timber many of the above natural defects can be eliminated when the process of conversion into scantling sizes is carried out, but warping and season checking can still occur. Warping and splitting are due mainly to the modern tendency to season and convert timber as quickly as possible. There is the tendency with logs sawn into planks, by slab cutting, for shrinkage to occur which warps the planks outwards away from the centre or heart. These defects adversely affect the structural strength of timber and this has led to the stress grading process for timber to be used in structural or load-bearing situations.

The weathering of timber has two main aspects, namely colour and moisture movement. Unless sealed and protected, timber exposed to the weather will change colour. Most dark timbers will bleach, whereas pale-coloured timbers often darken or redden slightly before losing the natural colour. Timber is hygroscopic and therefore in exposed conditions where it can get wet it will undergo changes in dimension, which are reversible as the timber dries out. The overall effect of dimensional fluctuations due to changes in moisture content is an eventual failure in fibre bonding resulting in splits and cracks, and with it a loss of strength. To reduce moisture movement to a minimum, timber should be specified with a moisture content in keeping with its intended use, but in no circumstances should this be in excess of 20 per cent since moisture contents above this figure create the conditions for fungal attack such as dry rot.

Timber is for all practical purposes an everlasting material and will not deteriorate unless attacked by some other agency such as fungi, insects or fire. Timber decays as a result of the destructive action of fungi growing on it, the most well known being called dry rot. True dry rot (*Merulius lacrymans*) requires a moisture content of about 20 per cent and once established can spread rapidly since behind its advance growth it forms water-conducting strands which enable it to adjust the moisture content of the timber to the optimum for itself. Wet rot requires a moisture content of about 30 per cent to become established and unlike dry rot is confined to the wet areas.

Insect infestation can also weaken and destroy timber in buildings and very often the damage has been done before it becomes apparent by the exit holes left behind by the emerging beetles. It is the wood-boring grubs which do the damage, by eating the timber fibres to extract the cellulose, rather than the adult beetle. Precautions to combat fungal and insect attack is by impregnation with suitable fungicides and insecticides, preferably before the timber is installed, and indeed in certain areas of England this is a Building Regulation requirement for structural roofing members. In the context of fungal attack the correct use of damp proof courses and surface treatments to maintain a low moisture content is also of paramount importance. The methods of recognition and treatment for infected timber in existing premises will be considered in the next chapter on causes and methods of repair.

Other timber products which should be considered consist mainly of cladding materials in the form of plywood, blockboard, laminboard, chipboard and fibreboard. It must be remembered that all the above products are produced from a natural material which retains its characteristics of moisture movement, the natural defects having been eliminated during the manufacturing processes. Apart from moisture movement consideration it is important that the right grade or quality is specified since most timber products are produced for either external and exposed conditions or for internal use and to use the latter in external situations could lead very quickly to an advanced state of deterioration due to a breakdown in the adhesives used in the manufacture of these products.

Concrete

Concrete is an artificial stone made by binding together coarse aggregates and fine aggregates or sand into a hard durable mass. The binding agent is one of the forms of cement available. When cement is mixed with water a chemical reaction is started which proceeds at a decreasing rate for some months, the finished product being ready for use within days or weeks depending on the strength requirement, mix design and curing conditions. Reinforced concrete is concrete where steel bars of an appropriate size and number have been fixed during construction in carefully designed and selected positions to increase the tensile and shearing strength of the concrete. By altering the ingredients of the mix either by type or amount it is possible to produce a wide range of concretes suitable for most situations.

The resistance of concrete to deterioration is therefore dependent on the quality of the materials used, the adequacy of the mix design and the quality of workmanship in mixing, placing, compacting and curing the concrete. Similarly the concrete's resistance to frost attack and subsequent spalling is dependent on the same factors. Concrete needs only a small water : cement ratio to promote the necessary chemical reaction but it would be unworkable if only the minimum amount of water was used; as the water content increases so does the workability and the permeability. If the latter is too high the concrete's resistance to frost and chemical attack diminishes as does the risk of corrosion of the reinforcement. Protection of the reinforcement is provided largely by the cover of concrete over the reinforcement and this should not be less than that recommended in table 19 of CP 110. The corrosion of the reinforcement could be accompanied by expansion of the metal which in turn could result in spalling or cracking. Minor corrosion can lead to disfiguring rust stains or streaks on the surface of the concrete. Chemical attack of concrete resulting in a complete breakdown of the mix is usually due to sulphates of calcium, magnesium and sodium which are very often present in clay subsoils. It is important therefore for the designer to be aware of their presence and specify the right type of cement together with the correct amount of concrete cover.

In terms of weathering, the major requirement is therefore to produce a concrete which has sufficient resistance to water and moisture penetration for the proposed situation. The mix design and workmanship should be carefully controlled to produce the desired result; however, cracking can occur and this will allow water or moisture to penetrate into the body of the concrete. Concrete shrinks as it sets and cures and if this is allowed to take place too quickly by being over exposed to drying winds and/or high temperatures during the initial curing stages the resultant shrinkage cracks could lead to deterioration at an early stage in the life of the concrete.

Concrete, like most other materials, will expand and contract with changes of temperature. The amount of movement which can be anticipated is governed by the mix design particularly with the chosen aggregate which will have a large influence on the concrete's coefficient of expansion. Two other important factors are the temperature range and the degree of exposure. The designer armed with the correct and accurate data can design concrete so as to minimize the effects of expansion which, if excessive, could lead to unacceptable cracking and/or spalling. Movement joints which are adequately sealed can also be incorporated in the overall design and detailed to allow the movement to take place without detriment to the concrete or the building as a whole.

Another aspect of the weathering of concrete is mainly concerned with appearance. It should be appreciated that the appearance of concrete can be greatly affected by the manner in which it is cast and not only by its subsequent exposure to the elements. The two main factors which affect its appearance are staining and surface growths:

1. *Staining:* when water in the form of rain strikes the face of concrete and runs down under gravitational force it can take with it any dirt or impurities present on the surface. This can result in a series of streaks due to the water drying out before it reaches the bottom of the unit or due to the impurities not being carried in suspension to the discharge edge. Staining is very often emphasized as a result of poor detailing; projections such as sills and copings will give a certain degree of protection from the rain and as a result discoloration beneath the overhang and unwashed area can become apparent. Careful detailing of surface texture and fenestration surrounds go a long way to avoiding some of the staining problems. Damp areas on the surface of exposed concrete can also give rise to surface growths.

2. *Surface growths:* these consist largely of algae, lichens and mosses which are usually green or red in colour, and like staining, are disfiguring rather than harmful. They can be killed by using toxic washes; whereas staining has to be cleaned off, and unless the cause is remedied the defect could well start up again after treatment or cleaning.

Glass

Glass is a very durable material made from soda, lime, silica and other minor ingredients such as magnesia and alumina, to produce a material suitable for general glazing of windows. Glass has great strength in compression but breaks under tension – the surface contains, so to speak, the strength; therefore any scoring of the surface will reduce its strength and possibly even breaking along the scored line.

The primary function of glass in windows is the transmission of natural daylight to the interior of the building whilst providing a suitable barrier to the elements. Approximately 90 per cent of the daylight which falls on the surface will be transmitted through the glass but unless the surface is kept clean this percentage will be reduced considerably. Glass in windows is usually in an exposed situation and therefore subject to high changes in temperature with its consequent thermal movement. If the window has been correctly detailed and installed this should present no problem since an adequate allowance should have been made in the housing or seating.

Glass, being brittle, will shatter easily upon impact, its strength being related to its size and thickness. In terms of wind pressure most manufacturers issue design guide charts showing the maximum sizes or dimensions for various types and thicknesses of glass related to an exposure index. In positions susceptible to vandalism toughened glass could be used; wired glass, contrary to popular belief, does not have a greater impact resistance to that of ordinary glass but should it become broken the embedded wire mesh will prevent the glass fragments from showering inwards, thus reducing the danger from flying glass. In these vulnerable areas polycarbonate plastic sheeting with its high-impact resistance could be considered as a suitable substitute for ordinary glass types.

Paint

Paint is a mixture of a liquid or medium and a colouring or pigment. Mediums used in paint manufacture range from thin liquids to stiff jellies and can be composed of linseed oil, drying oils, synthetic resins and water. The various combinations of these materials form the type or class of paint. The medium's function is to provide the means of spreading and binding the pigment over the surface to be painted. The pigment provides the body, colour and durability of the paint. The application of coats of paint to building elements, components, trims and fittings has two functions. The paint will impart colour and, at the same time, provide a protective coating which will increase the durability of the members to which it is applied.

Paint is one of the most vulnerable of all building materials and its need for regular maintenance resulting from either defects or weathering is one of the major items in any programme of maintenance. Defects in paintwork usually arise from one of the three following causes:

1. *Incorrect selection:* very often the prime concerns of the specifier of paint finishes is the colour, texture and appearance, which is of course one of the major reasons for choosing paint, but to obtain good durability as well as aesthetic appeal all paints must be selected in relationship to their exposure conditions and backing material or substrate.

2 *Application to damp surfaces:* entrapped moisture will in most cases affect the durability of a paint application by breaking down the adhesion or bond of the paint, causing flaking and cracking, which in turn will allow moisture

to enter and get between the paint and its backing, thus speeding up the deterioration.

3. Poor workmanship: this is probably one of the main causes of paint deterioration and defects and can usually be attributed to incorrect, inadequate or non-existent surface preparation, over-thinning of the paint, improper brush selection, poor brushing techniques and failing to apply the specified number of coats.

In all circumstances the recommendations of the paint manufacturer regarding selection, surface preparation and application should be followed. The Building Research Establishment Digests 197 and 198 give very good, clear and concise guidance as to the choice of paint and failures and remedies in the context of painting walls. Other digests deal with paint applications to timber and metals.

The deterioration of a paint may be visual or a breakdown of the material itself. Chemicals within the atmosphere, salt spray, daylight, sunlight and changes in temperature all play their part in the gradual but inevitable deterioration. A loss of colour or a loss of gloss is usually the first visible sign of weathering and if this weathering is allowed to continue the paint film will eventually become brittle, resulting in a loss of strength and cracking of the paint film. At an early stage it is usually possible to successfully maintain the paint surface by a simple rubbing down process form of surface preparation before applying new coats of paint. However, if redecoration is delayed too long and flaking is well advanced the surface preparation could entail removing all the existing paint layers down to the substrate before redecoration can be commenced and this is both costly and time consuming.

When paint has been specified to fulfil a primary function of protection, such as to ferrous metals in exposed conditions, the critical areas are the contact faces between the backing material and the paint. If this is good the paint will deteriorate by surface erosion, which is often called chalking, and not by loss of adhesion, cracking or flaking. The chief source of trouble is moisture, either from the rain or condensation, and to a large extent this can be minimized by good design and detailing which have been conceived to eliminate as far as possible areas where water might be trapped or condensation may persist. The bond may be regained on drying out but the continuous cycle of loss of adhesion and rebonding will lead ultimately to an irreversible breakdown of the paint film. This adhesion failure of paint can also be caused by differential movements of the paint and its backing due to changes in temperature.

It has already been stated that painting forms a large part of any maintenance programme and therefore building should be designed and constructed with this fact in mind. Future accessibility is often neglected in design considerations; fussy details making cleaning and surface preparation almost impossible once the component has been assembled and fixed are often incorporated into designs and details. It follows therefore that if a component cannot be adequately maintained the overall anticipated life of the building must diminish.

Asphalt and bitumen

Asphalt is a natural or manufactured mixture of bitumen with a substantial proportion of inert mineral matter. When heated, asphalt becomes plastic and can be moulded by hand into any shape. Bitumen is a complex mixture of hydrocarbons which has both waterproofing and adhesive properties. Bituminous-based materials have a very long natural life but this can be affected by sunlight, materials such as acids and fats and by impact damage.

When asphalt and bitumen are exposed to light and heat oxidation occurs; volatile and water-soluble degradation products are also formed which are removed by rain. This results in a slow hardening of the material, giving rise to cracking through thermal movements. Bitumen, being a thermoplastic material, will soften upon heating with a tendency to flow. In horizontal situations, such as an asphalt covering to a flat roof, an isolating membrane should be incorporated between the asphalt and the supporting structure to allow for differential movements. If this is omitted the continual expansion and contraction could result in the asphalt crack-ing, allowing moisture to penetrate. Heat can also cause entrapped air or moisture to expand beneath the impermeable asphalt layer which can cause blisters which when cooling and contracting split, thus allowing moisture to penetrate. Vertical applications should, however, have an adequately keyed surface to prevent flow of the asphalt as it softens with the rise in tempera-ture. To lessen the effects of sunlight and solar heat a reflective covering should be specified; this usually takes the form of a suitable light-coloured stone aggregate.

When set, mastic asphalt is brittle and can therefore be easily damaged by impact loadings and is most vulnerable during the construction stages of the building. It should be protected by a screed or similar coating if there is a risk of impact damage. Under permanent loadings bituminous base products can develop flow properties, reducing locally the protection being given, therefore heavy permanent loads should be fixed to and supported by suitable plinths unless a grade of material is selected which will adequately withstand this degree of loading. Bituminous felts behave in a similar manner to asphalt coverings with the possible exception of fire-resistant properties, but their durability depends mainly upon the properties of the base fabric which is impregnated by the bitumen rather than the bitumen itself.

We have therefore a selection of bitumen-based materials which have important properties for all concerned with building, but unless the design and workmanship are of a high standard the defects can be numerous and the deterioration not only of the material itself but also of the supporting structure can be very costly in terms of maintenance.

Plastics

The term plastic can be applied to any group of substances based on syn-thetic or modified natural polymers which during manufacture are moulded by heat or pressure or both into any form. They are used extensively in the building industry in both the thermoplastic and thermosetting forms. Contrary to popular belief, plastics are not new to the building industry, bakelite having been used successfully for many years, but the last decades have seen a rapid rise in the number of plastics and applications available. The plastics of today give the designer and builder a group of materials which are strong, reasonably durable, easy to assemble and fit, low maintenance and, since they lend themselves to mass production, of an acceptable cost.

To fully understand, appreciate and utilize the many plastics available the designer would need to have the knowledge of a qualified chemist, therefore plastics are generally specified by their overall grouping such as polyvinyl chloride (PVC). It must be appreciated that a plastic within a general grouping can be formulated to change some of the specific properties such as its reaction to ultra violet light. A practical example within the same group is opaque PVC for rainwater goods and translucent PVC for rooflight sheeting. It follows therefore, as with other materials, that incorrect selection or specification can lead to deterioration of the chosen material if used in unfavourable situations.

Generally plastics formulated for external applications weather very well since they have a very low water absorption and are not damaged to a great extent by exposure to water. Most plastics are self coloured, albeit in a limited range, and therefore do not require decoration for appearance or protection but exposure to sunlight and general weather conditions can lead to a certain degree of discoloration. Temperature changes can also cause some plastics to soften and others to become brittle, but providing their individual properties are appreciated in terms of support and protection requirements most plastics will give a satisfactory service with low maintenance costs over some thirty years or more.

Mastics and sealants

With the trend in many modern buildings and structures to use large prefabricated cladding units the normal small unit joint sealers such as cement and gauge mortars are unacceptable since they cannot accommodate the movements associated with these larger units. Any material used for joint sealing whether in the context of complex claddings or gap filling between a simple frame and its opening must fulfil the following requirements:

1. Provide a weather-tight seal.
2. Accommodate all anticipated movements such as thermal, structural and moisture movements.
3. Accommodate and mask tolerance variations.
4. Remain stable.
5. Should not give rise to the staining of other materials.

There are many mastics and sealants available to fulfil the above requirements with a wide range of costs, properties and life expectancies. The life of these sealants ranges from ten to twenty-five years, which in most cases is less than the anticipated life of the surrounding materials and components, therefore all joints should be designed in such a manner that they can be maintained or renewed with reasonable ease, efficiency and cost. Mastics are materials which are applied in a plastic state and form a surface skin over the core which remains pliable for a number of years. They are generally cheaper than sealants but will not accept the same degree of movement and usually have a shorter anticipated life. Sealants are applied in a plastic state and are converted by chemical reactions into an elastomer or synthetic rubber.

The weathering of mastics and sealants depends largely upon the type and formulation of the material but generally there is a tendency for most plastics to harden and/or craze with age, thus losing some of their movement accommodation properties or allowing moisture to penetrate. The amount of dirt pick-up leading to discoloration is also a variable factor of the different types.

Sealants which deteriorate rapidly or become defective are usually incorrectly specified, detailed or poorly applied. It cannot be overstressed that correct specifying and detailing in terms of gap width, minimum depth, adhesive properties, material and surface preparation are of the utmost importance if a successful joint is to be achieved. It follows that correct procedures must also be carried out on site to fulfil the designer's requirements and objectives, since if either party is at fault the consequences can be far reaching because the failure of a mastic or sealant in a joint can allow some of the elements to penetrate into the building, causing deterioration of the internal materials.

Fire factors

Fire, if uncontrolled, can be a hazard to both the building and the persons within the building but before a fire can start there must be the three essentials present, namely:

1. *Fuel:* generally any organic material is suitable.

2. *Heat:* this must be at the correct temperature to promote combustion of any particular fuel.

3. *Oxygen:* air is necessary to sustain and support the combustion process.

Materials used in building are usually classified as being combustible or non-combustible, the latter being any material which will not burn or give off sufficient quantity of inflammable vapour to cause ignition. Components and building elements are tested to establish their degree of fire resistance which is usually measured in hours or parts of hours. All materials and components can be adversely affected by fire either directly by being wholly or partially consumed, by losing some of its properties, particularly structural strength, or by losing its aesthetic appeal.

At the design stage the designer must consider what materials or components are suitable for any particular situation in terms of inherent fire resistance or the degree of fire protection required. He must also consider what would be the consequences of a fire should it occur in terms of what materials are likely to be affected, how will they be affected, and what reaction is there likely to be from other materials not directly involved in the fire but affected by the heat of a nearby fire. The aftermath of a fire must also be considered since a great deal of damage can be done by the firefighters in their efforts to control the fire. Water used during the fire fighting can not only damage but also set up deterioration in materials not directly involved. The heat and also the combination of heat and water can also lead to the swelling, distortion, spalling and cracking of nearby materials and components. In terms of maintenance the examination of a building after a fire for evidence and signs of deterioration and defects must be very thorough and not confined solely to the materials and components in the immediate vicinity of the fire.

Chapter 6

Causes and methods of repair, renewal and alterations

All forms of maintenance and alteration work carry an element of risk of damage to one's own property, adjoining properties and to injury to persons. If the work is being carried out by direct works labour then the onus is on the employer to see that he is covered by his insurance for the extra risks created by maintenance and adaptation works, and for any third party claims which may arise because of these operations. If the work is to be undertaken by an independent contractor then the terms of the contract could shift the onus on to the maintenance contractor but it is still a wise precaution to take out an adequate insurance to cover all third party liabilities irrespective of who is negligent. This insurance should be in the joint names of the employer and contractor. Another reason for taking out such insurances is that by a study of the legal requirements contained in such documents as the Health and Safety at Work, etc. Act, Factories Acts, Offices, Shops and Railway Premises Act and the Construction Regulations it will be seen that there can be a conflict as to responsibility for providing and maintaining adequate temporary support and protection during building works, therefore should any problem of responsibility arise as a result of the works it could lead to complex legal arguments before a satisfactory conclusion is achieved.

Temporary protection and support

When undertaking any form of maintenance, extension or adaptation work the question of temporary protection and support must be considered at an early stage, indeed in some cases this will be part of the feasibility study. This may involve the need to seek the opinion and advice of a specialist such as a structural engineer. These two aspects can be considered separately but very often they will have to work in conjunction with one another.

Temporary protection

The first question to ask under this heading is: who or what is to be protected? If the premises are furnished and occupied then consideration must be given to protecting the furniture, finishes and fittings which cannot be removed whilst the works are being carried out. This could range from a simple dust sheet covering over floor finishes and furniture to a protective screen of traditional studwork construction covered with a suitable facing material such as plastic, hardboard or fibreboard. This form of protecting screen is primarily intended to keep out the dust created by the works in progress but it can have a secondary function of providing some degree of sound insulation or providing a barrier to eliminate the visual distraction. Temporary protection may also be needed for such items as fireplace surrounds and this can be achieved by forming a freestanding enclosure of small sized timbers, using the studwork principles, around the projection and covering the framework with a suitable material which will keep out the dust and resist any likely impact.

If the works are external such as façade cleaning operations, the adjacent walls and the general public may well need protecting. This form of temporary protection is normally incorporated in the access scaffold design by using attached lining material and double boarding techniques. The operatives, apart from the protection afforded by the scaffold, may have to be supplied with protective clothing. Work which involves structural alterations should be surrounded by a close boarded hoarding constructed in accordance with the licence issued by the local authority; it may also be necessary to provide a gantry platform and/or a fan hoarding. Students at this level of study should be familiar with the details of the above mentioned scaffolds and hoarding and in this context it is usually a matter of simple adaptation to provide the necessary temporary protection by this type of work as opposed to new constructional work.

Temporary support

This can take the form of a simple steel adjustable prop to a complex system of shoring to give the necessary temporary support to the surroundings or adjacent structure whilst the remedial or adaptation works are being carried out. Unless the need for temporary support is of a simple nature, such as supporting a domestic floor by using timber head and sole plates in conjunction with vertical props, a structural survey should be carried out. This is needed to assess the support required in terms of type and strength and also to ascertain the strength and condition of the existing elements. The reasons for the survey are important and must be defined so that the right information is collected and recorded. If the temporary support is required because of a defect then the cause of the defect may well have a direct bearing on the type and amount of temporary support to be given to enable the remedial work to proceed safely and unhindered by badly positioned or inadequate supports. If temporary support is required for alterations, extension or adaptation work the strength of the existing structure may have to be assessed to see if it will safely accept extra loadings, thrusts or forces.

With remedial work the first evidence which usually indicates a defect or failure is cracking. Cracks occurring in the finishes are common particularly where the finish is covering a joint between brickwork and timber, such as over a bedded wall plate; if the width of the crack along its length does not exceed 2 mm it is usually due to shrinkage and can be made good with fillers prior to decorating. To establish that cracks like this are due to shrinkage and not the beginnings of serious structural movement, they can be monitored by using studs and calipers, feeler gauges or reference lines. In all cases the reading must be accurately taken and recorded. If it is established that the cracking is due to movement of the building the temporary support in the form of hydraulic jacks, simple props or in extreme cases shoring may have to be used to stop further movement, enable the cause to be investigated and the remedial work to be undertaken.

In the case of extension and adaptation work a structural survey should be carried out to establish the strength of existing elements and what support will be required during the proposed works. The survey should be detailed and carried out to ascertain which are the structural or load-bearing members; this may mean the removal of finishes, particularly at junctions. If the building contains structural members of concrete or steelwork the advice of a qualified structural engineer should be sought and it may be necessary to extract core samples for analysis and testing to establish true strength properties.

Once the survey is complete the position of any temporary supports can be determined by using the survey in conjunction with the proposed project details and specification. Sizing, spacing and types of support required can be found by using basic structural design principles or, if using traditional materials, by rules of thumb or empirical methods which are given in many textbooks such as those on carpentry and joinery. For typical protection and simple support example see Fig. 6.1. The amount of consideration and planning which can be given to protection and support will depend upon the urgency of the work.

Types of maintenance

Maintenance can be defined as any work undertaken in order to keep or restore every part of a building to an acceptable standard. The type of maintenance work needed to achieve this objective will depend upon whether the work was planned or unplanned. A well run establishment will have planned for all maintenance in accordance with the resources available and the standards they wish to set. The alternative is to wait until replacement or repair is imperative or until its efficiency falls below an acceptable level. The danger in adopting this alternative is that it could lead to the need for emergency maintenance.

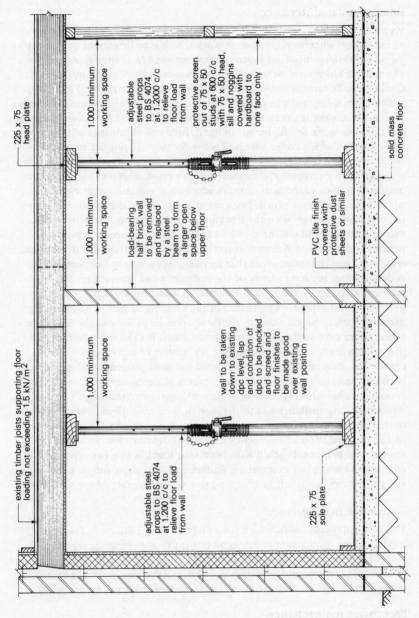

Fig. 6.1. Typical example of simple protection and support measures

Emergency maintenance

Maintenance which needs to be carried out immediately is called emergency maintenance, whereas maintenance work which is to be carried out or implemented within twenty-four hours is often referred to as urgent maintenance. The test for emergency or urgent considerations is to pose the question, Could there be serious consequences in the context of structural stability, health risks, safety risks to persons or to adjoining or neighbouring properties? If the answer is yes to any of these aspects then the urgent or emergency maintenance work should be put in hand, firstly to eliminate the serious consequences which could arise and secondly to carry out the necessary corrective maintenance.

Emergency maintenance is something to avoid wherever and whenever possible but even in the best of establishments it can still occur especially where services are concerned. For example, a nearby gas explosion due to a fractured main can weaken the structure, causing damage to such items as external finishes and glazing which in turn can be dangerous to nearby persons and can cause discomfort to those within the premises. If a service is at fault then the isolation of that service is of paramount importance. A detailed and accurate survey of the premises or of any part of the premises affected by the fault is essential to assess the need for temporary protection and support. Evacuation of the building or part of the building may also have to be considered. All these considerations and the resultant action taken may well result in unplanned costs. It cannot be overstressed that whatever the cause of the emergency, expert advice is required and required quickly; therefore some form of standard procedure should have been planned such as the telephone numbers of various experts should be available without having to resort to a prolonged search through various directories; responsibilities as to decision making must be clearly defined so that any confusion as to an instruction's validity can be avoided; access to and the operation of emergency cut-outs should be clearly marked and known, and personnel should have been instructed as to what action to take in the event of an emergency. Failure to adopt these simple precautions and procedures can result in chaos, panic and a worsening of the situation.

Corrective maintenance

This is maintenance work which is carried out after a failure has occurred and can range from a simple fuse replacement to the complete replacement of a major component. For obvious reasons this form of maintenance should be avoided wherever and whenever possible and the best method of minimizing corrective maintenance is a system of preventive maintenance.

Preventive maintenance

Basically this is any maintenance carried out in the anticipation of a failure. A flushing cistern which does not activate every time the lever is depressed will eventually fail to work unless maintained to prevent this occurring; a door which is sticking could well become permanently closed unless preventive measures are undertaken; loose fittings may become detached unless action is taken to resecure them; unless missing or loose roofing tiles are replaced or refixed further tiles could be dislodged by wind action or the elements could enter the roof space, causing more damage. Many more examples of preventive maintenance could be given as illustrations but they would only emphasize the point already made, that if something is wrong it will almost certainly get worse unless some form of preventive work is carried out.

Planned maintenance

This is a definite programme of maintenance work with the objective of reducing to a minimum the need for corrective or emergency maintenance. The maintenance schedules used would indicate the time intervals at which certain maintenance items will be carried out. These schedules could include actual work items such as the annual servicing of boilers and redecoration programmes; they could also include testing and inspection procedures to see if preventive maintenance is required and they could indicate the replacement life cycle of specific items.

A planned maintenance programme will make the most efficient use of resources such as men and equipment. It will enable the work load of maintenance staff to be planned for both direct and contract labour and it will also enable an economic policy of stock holding to be formulated. Planned maintenance may also bring other benefits such as improved safety measures, higher morale of the workforce due to less disturbance and frustration caused by breakdowns and this could result in higher productivity. However, any form of planned maintenance should have a degree of flexibility within its formulation, otherwise unnecessary maintenance may be carried out such as replacing items which still have useful life left in them because their anticipated life span has expired, and redecorating clean areas because the five-year planned life has expired.

Before any maintenance work can be put in hand, decisions as to what, when and how must be taken. It is impossible to list and describe every form of maintenance which could arise but the following examples of causes and remedies will serve to emphasize the procedure of diagnosing the cause, deciding the remedial work to be undertaken, carrying out the work and recording the findings and action taken in the form of feedback information to be used in future design and planning exercises. For summary of maintenance types see Fig. 6.2.

Dampness within buildings

Dampness in buildings, particularly those of a domestic nature, is a constant source of trouble. It causes rapid deterioration of many materials and can create the conditions favourable for fungal and insect attack. It is essential in all cases to establish the cause of the problem before carrying out any maintenance work to make the building dry. Dampness can arise from a variety of sources including rain penetration, rising damp, faulty plumbing and condensation.

114

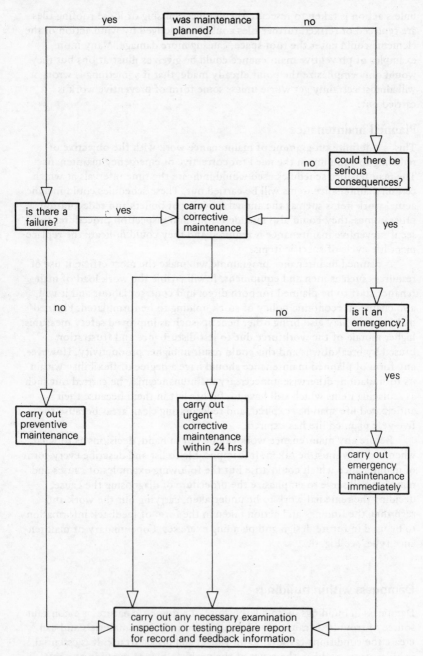

Fig. 6.2. Summary of types of maintenance

115

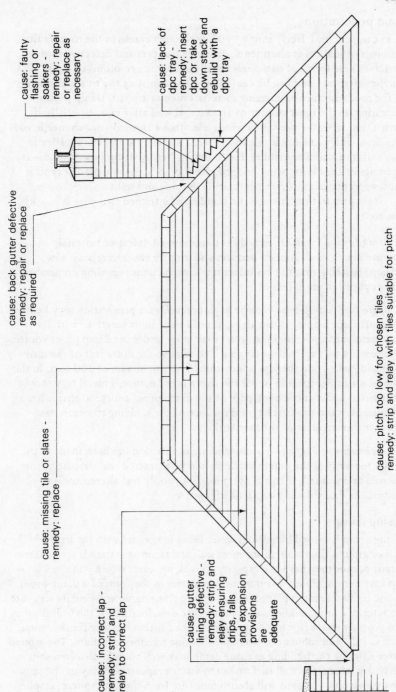

cause: faulty flashing or soakers - remedy: repair or replace as necessary

cause: lack of dpc tray - remedy: insert dpc or take down stack and rebuild with a dpc tray

cause: back gutter defective remedy: repair or replace as required

cause: missing tile or slates - remedy: replace

cause: pitch too low for chosen tiles - remedy: strip and relay with tiles suitable for pitch

cause: incorrect lap - remedy: strip and relay to correct lap

cause: gutter lining defective - remedy: strip and relay ensuring drips, falls and expansion provisions are adequate

Fig. 6.3. Rain penetration — pitched roofs and chimneys

Rain penetration

Rain can penetrate freely into a building through cracks in the roof, faulty flashings or soakers at abutments, defective parapets and defective roof gutters. These forms of dampness usually show the symptoms of damp patches after rain and can be caused by a single missing tile to serious defects in the roof structure of covering materials such as asphalt. Damp patches appearing on the inner surface of an external wall after rain, especially if such a wall faces the prevailing wind, are often a common occurrence in old buildings with a one-brick thick solid wall. Buildings with cavity walls can also suffer in a similar manner due to unsatisfactory damp-proof courses at openings or the cavity being bridged. See Figs. 6.3, 6.4 and 6.5 for typical causes and remedies of rain penetration in roofs and walls.

Rain penetration through the cladding of a framed structure is usually due to:

1. Breakdown of sealant: remedy is to remove all defective material, thoroughly clean all contact surfaces and prepare them to receive new sealant, ensuring that the manufacturer's instructions regarding preparation and application are followed.

2. Inadequate damp-proof course at floor level: rain penetration may be due to insufficient lapping of the damp-proof course in its length or with its abutment with the column or water may enter under the damp-proof course. The remedy for insufficient lapping is to remove the outer leaf of the cladding and make good the laps which should be a minimum of 100 mm. In the case of water penetration under the damp-proof course, a metal tray should be inserted under the leading edge of the damp-proof course so that it has an adequate lap and projects beyond the face of the cladding to ensure rainwater is thrown clear of the facework.

3. Breakdown of baffle in a drained joint: if provision has been made in the design for renewal the defect baffle should be extracted and a replacement inserted and secured. If this is not possible the only real alternative is to convert the drained joint into a filled joint.

Rising damp

Rising damp is caused by ground water being in contact with the base of a wall or ground floor slab. Since most wall and flooring materials are to some extent porous they have the capacity to soak up water which will rise by capillary action. Unless an impermeable barrier in the form of a damp-proof course or membrane is placed in its path the rising damp will find its way into the interior of the building, which can cause deterioration of the wall finishes and possibly encourage mould growth. In the context of floor finishes some such as PVC and rubber can become loose due to adhesive failure. The ground water entering the building as rising damp may well contain dissolved salts which are left on the wall surface as the water evaporates. Many of the salts are hygroscopic and thus will absorb moisture from the atmosphere, amplifying the damp areas. Any wall finishes affected in this manner should be

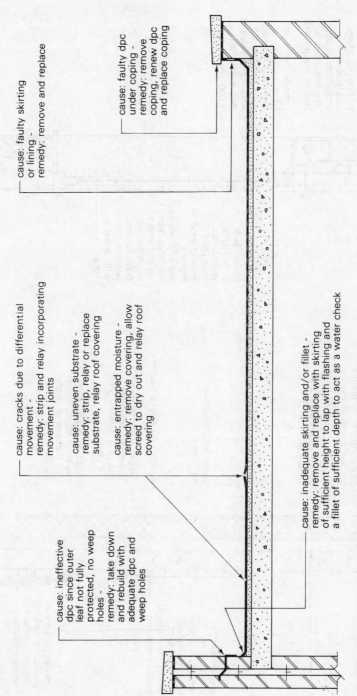

cause: faulty skirting or lining -
remedy: remove and replace

cause: faulty dpc under coping -
remedy: remove coping, renew dpc and replace coping

cause: cracks due to differential movement -
remedy: strip and relay incorporating movement joints

cause: uneven substrate -
remedy: strip, relay or replace substrate, relay roof covering

cause: entrapped moisture -
remedy: remove covering, allow screed to dry out and relay roof covering

cause: inadequate skirting and/or fillet -
remedy: remove and replace with skirting of sufficient height to lap with flashing and a fillet of sufficient depth to act as a water check

cause: ineffective dpc since outer leaf not fully protected, no weep holes -
remedy: take down and rebuild with adequate dpc and weep holes

Fig. 6.4. Rain penetration – flat roofs and parapets

118

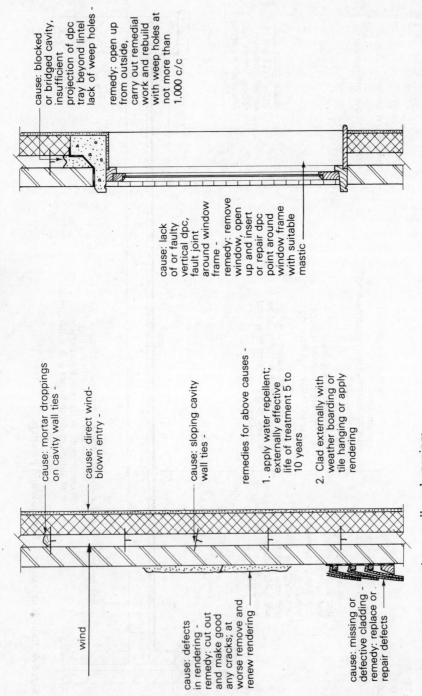

cause: blocked
or bridged cavity,
insufficient
projection of dpc
tray beyond lintel
lack of weep holes -

remedy: open up
from outside,
carry out remedial
work and rebuild
with weep holes at
not more than
1.000 c/c

cause: lack
of or faulty
vertical dpc,
fault joint
around window
frame -
remedy: remove
window, open
up and insert
or repair dpc
point around
window frame
with suitable
mastic

cause: mortar droppings
on cavity wall ties -

cause: direct wind-
blown entry -

cause: sloping cavity
wall ties -

remedies for above causes -

1. apply water repellent;
externally effective
life of treatment 5 to
10 years

2. Clad externally with
weather boarding or
tile hanging or apply
rendering

wind

cause: defects
in rendering -
remedy: cut out
and make good
any cracks; at
worse remove and
renew rendering

cause: missing or
defective cladding -
remedy: replace or
repair defects

Fig. 6.5. Rain penetration — walls and openings

removed and replaced after any remedial treatment has been carried out.

The way to combat rising damp is to remove the cause if the damp-proof course is being by-passed or to insert a barrier if there is not one present. The barrier can take the form of a damp-proof course which is installed by cutting into a horizontal joint with a special saw, inserting wedges to take the load and finally inserting the damp-proof course material. Alternatives are injecting a water-repellant substance into the wall such as a siliconate solution in water or a silicon/latex mixture; or by installing a system of electro-osmosis which works on the principle of water moving between sources of different electric potential.

The above methods of eradicating rising damp can be expensive and may involve drying out the walls after treatment before the interior is free of dampness. An alternative approach is to accept the rising damp within the walls and place a vertical barrier between the damp wall and the interior of the building, since dampness in the wall is not likely to give rise to any structural problems; the only real defect to overcome is the damp penetration into the building. A suitable barrier can be constructed by using any dry lining technique which has an impermeable property such as foil or polythene-backed plasterboard fixed to wall battens, which have been treated with a fungicide to prevent mould growth within the new cavity. This method, in common with other lining methods, such as a bitumen-impregnated lathing fixed to the wall and covered with a traditional plaster finish, will diminish slightly the internal dimensions of the rooms involved but as a bonus it may well improve the thermal insulating properties of the wall. For typical causes and remedies of rising damp see Fig. 6.6.

Faulty plumbing

A burst pipe is usually discovered at an early stage since this normally gives both a visual and audible indication of the fault. The only remedy is to turn off the supply, drain down the service if necessary and renew the length of pipe in which the fault has occurred. Investigation as to the cause should also be undertaken and if this was due to freezing the pipe should be well lagged or re-routed to a less vulnerable position. Leaks from joints and traps due to faulty workmanship, faulty materials or to metal fatigue caused by repetitive expansion and contraction are not so obvious since the leakage could be very slight and many of the joints and traps are in hidden positions. The first signs of a leakage are very often the appearance of damp patches on walls, floors or ceilings. Again the remedy is to isolate the supply, drain down if required and remake, repair or replace the faulty joint or trap.

Condensation

Condensation is one of the major problems in buildings, especially in dwellings designed and constructed without an open fireplace which in older properties acted as a source of ventilation, extracting the moisture-laden air which is replaced by drier air. Condensation occurs when warm moist air comes into contact with a cold surface. Warm air has the ability to hold moisture, the amount varying with the temperature, so if the temperature

Nature of condensation

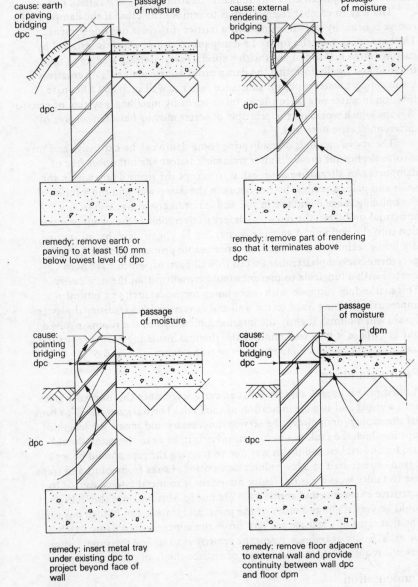

cause: earth or paving bridging dpc

passage of moisture

dpc

remedy: remove earth or paving to at least 150 mm below lowest level of dpc

cause: external rendering bridging dpc

passage of moisture

dpc

remedy: remove part of rendering so that it terminates above dpc

cause: pointing bridging dpc

passage of moisture

dpc

remedy: insert metal tray under existing dpc to project beyond face of wall

cause: floor bridging dpc

passage of moisture

dpm

dpc

remedy: remove floor adjacent to external wall and provide continuity between wall dpc and floor dpm

Fig. 6.6. Rising damp – typical causes and remedies

of the air decreases, as when it meets a cold surface, its ability to hold a certain amount of moisture diminishes. When warm air is holding its maximum amount of water for a particular temperature it is said to be saturated and the temperature at which this occurs is called the dewpoint temperature since any lowering of the temperature will cause some of the moisture to condense in the form of droplets of water. If the air in contact with the cold surface is not saturated it will, as the cooling effect continues, reach its dewpoint or saturation temperature and condensation will occur.

Condensation which occurs on the surface and is visual is called 'surface condensation', whereas condensation which occurs within the body of the material or component is called 'interstitial condensation', and providing the conditions of moisture-laden air reaching its dewpoint temperature or lower are present, condensation will occur in either form. To control and thus remedy the problem of condensation three aspects, namely ventilation, heating and thermal insulation, must be considered.

1. Ventilation: this can help to reduce condensation by allowing warm moist air to escape and drier air to enter; however, these air movements can produce draughts and also there could be a drop in temperature. A balance of air exchange with temperature drop is therefore required. In situations where a great deal of moisture is produced, such as in bathrooms and kitchens, it may be necessary to install a powered extract fan to remove the moisture-laden air quickly. The most effective method is to have a ducted system incorporating an extract fan with inlets over the moisture-generating appliances, the duct being taken and directly connected to the external air.

2. Heating: the contribution of heating to counteract condensation is two-fold. First, the heating will warm up the surrounding air, and second, it will warm up the general fabric of the premises to above dewpoint. To warm up the fabric to the right temperature takes time and this objective is very seldom satisfactorily achieved by a system of intermittent heating; this is especially true in very cold weather. The high cost of fuels and the fact that many premises are unoccupied for many hours of each day tends to make intermittent heating an attractive proposition. Once the fabric has been warmed up it can normally be maintained at that temperature by a continuous low heat input since it does not lose heat rapidly by radiation as is the case with intermittent heating. Heaters which produce water as a by-product of the combustion process such as flueless paraffin heaters should not be used in rooms or situations prone to condensation problems.

3. Thermal insulation: the objective of thermal insulation is to reduce the heat loss through a member thus making its surface warmer. The insulation should be placed on the inside or warm side of the wall and must be carefully chosen and installed. The air which will come in contact with the insulating material could be moist and if this moisture is absorbed by the insulating material its insulating properties could diminish, therefore the inclusion of an impermeable vapour barrier on the warm side of the insulating material must be considered. Other methods of thermal insulation include filling the cavity with special foams, double glazing to windows and the use of reflective materials.

It must be understood that in situations where condensation is occurring it is unlikely that the problem can be remedied by any one of the above methods of control; a suitable combination is usually required. If the heating output in the affected area is improved then there must be an adequate means of ventilation to allow the warm moist air to escape, similarly there is no point in thermally insulating walls when there is little or no heat input.

Condensation can also be a problem in unventilated roof spaces where thermal insulating material has been placed at ceiling level. The remedy is to ventilate the roof by the introduction of air through the eaves soffit board. A rule of thumb guide is to allow 300 mm^2 of free opening for every 300 mm of eaves run. This will result in an increase in heat loss from the roof of approximately 5 to 10 per cent but condensation in the roof space can lower the value of insulating material should it become damp and also it can increase the moisture content of the timbers to an unacceptable level. Any services within the roof space should be well lagged or protected against becoming frozen.

The calculations which are necessary to ascertain the best remedy in any given situation where condensation has occurred or is likely to occur are beyond the scope of this text but such data is available from Building Research Establishment Digests, textbooks and manufacturers' literature dealing with various aspects of this topic. Condensation will often promote mould growth on the damp surfaces and this must be treated with a suitable fungicide after the remedial work has been carried out.

Dry and wet rot

Dry rot (*Merulius lacrymans*)

This is a species of fungi which cause decay in timbers. This fungus rapidly consumes the woody tissue, the affected parts ultimately becoming dark brown, dry and powdery, with splits both along and across the grain. There is often the appearance of a fine red dust and a damp musty smell. A certain degree of moisture is essential to the growth of the fungus; the timber must have a moisture content of over 20 per cent. It must be appreciated that once established the fungus can spread through dry areas such as walls and attack dry timbers, since the conducting strands put out by the fungus enable it to adjust the moisture content of the wood.

A single plant of a dry rot fungus puts forth millions of reproductive spores which, being of microscopic size, may be borne about by the air, conveyed imperceptibly from infected timber to sound timber on shoes and clothing, or the decay can be spread by the dispersion of infected sawdust or by bridging some other material from which the fungus can derive no sustenance as described above.

An attack of dry rot can be recognized by the affected timber being covered in prolific mycelial (thread-like) growth ranging from a white to

yellow to grey coloured strands. Fruiting bodies attached to w
may also be seen, particularly if the attack is well advanced. Th
bodies are fleshy, soft and shaped like a pancake with white edg
yellow to brick red centre from which the spores are released.

Before any remedial work is undertaken the extent and cause o ...ie
outbreak must be established: this could involve the removal of floors, wall
finishes and trims. Common causes of the dampness which allows dry rot to
propagate are blocked air bricks to a suspended timber floor, defective drains
and gullies, bridged damp-proof courses, broken or missing roof tiles or slates
and leakages from faulty plumbing. The cause, having been found, should be
rectified and/or repaired as necessary. All infected timber should be cut out
and burned immediately, and the timber should be cut at least 600 mm
beyond the infected area to ensure that all traces of the fungus have been
destroyed. All infected wall finishes such as plaster should be removed and
destroyed, again going beyond the area of attack by at least 600 mm.

All walls which are near to the infected timbers should be sterilized by
heat such as a blowlamp and then treated with a suitable fungicide before the
new timber is installed. In cases of severe outbreaks some fungicide manufacturers recommend sterilization of the walls by means of irrigation which
entails drilling small diameter holes at specified centres and filling these with
the fungicide. All replacement timber should be well seasoned and treated
with a preservative; all remaining sound timber should receive *in situ* preservative treatment. In all cases the manufactuer's advice and instructions should
be followed if subsequent outbreaks are to be avoided. Many manufacturers
of preservatives and fungicide will carry out all the remedial work and give
an extensive guarantee of their work and against further fungal attack.

Wet rot

Wet rot is a collective term for wood-destroying fungi other than the dry rot
described above. These fungi require very wet conditions in which to germi-
nate, usually in excess of 30 per cent moisture content. Wet rot can occur
both indoors and outdoors and is more common in its occurrence than dry
rot, but the attacks are seldom as extensive or serious as dry rot. They are
confined to the actual damp areas since they do not have the ability to
spread to sound timbers in the same manner as dry rot. The procedure of
finding the cause of the dampness, curing the cause and replacing all affected
timber with sound timber treated with a preservative are as described above
for dry rot but in this case it is only necessary to remove the infected timber
and not the sound timber on either side. As with dry rot, all the sound
timber in the vicinity should be treated with suitable timber preservative.

The recognition of the two common forms of wet rot are given below;
the eradication treatment is common to both types.

1. Cellar fungus (Coniphora cerebella): this fungus will attack both hardwoods and softwoods and requires very damp conditions. There is very often
no visible external growth or fruiting bodies but sometimes blackish brown
thread-like strands can be seen on the surface. The affected timber usually

...urns dark brown with longitudinal cracking. Sometimes cross grain cracking occurs below a surface veneer of sound wood.

2. *Mine fungus* (Poria vaillantii): this fungus attacks softwoods in very damp situations. The surface appearance consists of pure white twine-like strands which remain flexible when dried. The fruiting bodies consist of flat white plates with visible white pores. The affected timber is usually light brown in colour with grain cracks similar to that of dry rot but less pronounced and usually less extensive.

No form of wet or dry rot should be ignored. The cause must be found and eradicated and the affected timber removed and replaced as described above. If any doubt as to identification and treatment exists, specialist advice should be sought at the earliest possible stage.

Insect infestation

Insect infestation of timber can range from an isolated incident to serious outbreak requiring drastic remedial measures. In most cases the damage has been done before it becomes evident, since it is the grubs or larvae which eat the timber causing the damage and it is the emerging beetles leaving behind their exit holes and the dust-like refuse expelled from the boreholes. The various species have differences in appearance and habitats but the life cycle is the same for all the major species which attack timbers in buildings.

The life cycle commences with the female beetle laying a number of eggs in cracks in timber, open joints on a rough timber surface, and old exit or flight holes. Within a few weeks the larvae or grubs are hatched and commence boring into the timber. The grubs, which are often referred to as woodworms, eat all the timber substance in front of them, digesting the food content and excreting the unwanted material behind them in a distinctive form of dust-like particles. The grubs remain active in the timber for a number of years after which they pupate in the form of a chrysalis near to the surface of the timber. Within a few weeks the adult beetle emerges and mates, usually within hours. The male beetle dies after mating but the female survives long enough to lay her eggs and so recommence the life cycle. The beetles, which are capable of flight, usually emerge in the warm weather between April and August.

An attack by wood-boring insects is easily distinguished from other forms of timber deterioration by the distinctive exit or flight holes and, if recent, by the dust-like particles. The adult beetles of the different species can also be easily identified as shown in Fig. 6.7. After identification the remedial work is to:

1. Cut away and burn badly attacked timber.
2. Examine all timber in the vicinity for evidence of infestation. This may require the lifting of floor boards, taking down of panelling and the removal of surface finishes such as paint.
3. Assess the structural strength of any remaining timber and take remedial action in accordance with findings.

Common furniture beetle
(Anobium punctatum)

length: 6-8 mm
colour: dark brown
bore dust: fine sand-like particles
exit holes: circular approximately 1.5 mm diameter
number of eggs: 20-40; maximum 80
hatching time: 4 to 5 weeks
life cycle: 2 or more years
attacks: hardwoods and softwoods; favours old
    timber

Death watch beetle
(Xestobium rufovillosum)

length: 8-12 mm
colour: dark brown, can be mottled
bore dust: bun-shaped, approximately
     1.0 mm diameter
exit hole: circular, approximately 3 mm diameter
number of eggs: 40 to 70
hatching time: 2 to 8 weeks
life cycle: 4 to 10 years
attacks: hardwoods especially after fungal decay

House longhorn beetle
(Hylotrupes bajculus)

length: 15-25 mm
colour: brown or black with shiny black
    spots behind head
bore dust: fine dust and barrel-shaped pellets
exit hole: oblique slits not clear-cut holes
number of eggs: up to 200
hatching time: 2 to 4 weeks
life cycle: 3 to 11 years
attacks: softwood especially in roofs
    (rare in UK except for parts of Surrey)

Powder post beetle
*(Lyctus and other
species)*

length: 6-8 mm
colour: reddish-brown
bore dust: very fine dust
exit hole: circular, approximately 1.5 mm diameter
number of eggs: 70 to 200
hatching time: 2 to 3 weeks
life cycle: 1 to 2 years
attacks: sapwood of hardwood within 15 years of
    felling

Fig. 6.7. Wood-boring insects

4. Ensure that all new and existing timbers are treated with a suitable insecticide in accordance with the manufacturer's recommendations.

It is a wise precaution when specifying timber for any new work to have this impregnated with an insecticide and also a fungicide to prevent attacks of this nature.

Assessing maintenance needs

When a defect manifests itself the temptation is to immediately order and carry out remedial work, and in simple cases such as replacing a tap washer or a simple fixture such as a broken coat hook this is all that is normally required, but in most cases an investigation should be carried out to find the cause and source of the defect. Any investigation should be undertaken without any preconceived ideas and with the utmost care since it may be necessary to remove parts of the fabric to ascertain the cause and this, if carelessly carried out, could destroy the evidence sought.

The amount of time and money which can be expended on such an investigation will depend upon such factors as urgency, extent of defect, structural or non-structural, reason for investigation such as finding a suitable remedy or who is liable and whether the fault is of a well known or common nature. The equipment required can range from a simple rule to moisture meters and equipment for taking core samples for laboratory analysis.

The first objective of an investigation is to find the primary cause of the defect since there may be several contributory causes. A damp patch may be the defect which is caused by rain penetrating through a crack in the external fabric which could be caused by a movement in the foundations due to a shrinkable clay subsoil. Does the remedial treatment consist of filling the crack and/or underpinning the foundations? This is what the investigation must establish. There are basically only three causes of defects and these are:

1. Dampness.
2. Movements.
3. Chemical/biological changes.

All of the above causes can have many sources and it is usually these sources which need to be eliminated in any remedial works to prevent the defect recurring.

Principal sources of defects

Dampness

The principal sources of dampness defects in buildings can be listed as follows:

1. Rain penetration: either into the body of the fabric, to internal finishes by percolation or capillary action or by direct entry through gaps and holes.

2. Ground sources: usually shows in the form of rising damp which can result from very wet or waterlogged ground around the foundations, underground floors and in the vicinity of basements.

3. Atmospheric sources: this can be any form of pollution over which there is no method of control and the defect is the result of poor material specification; condensation is another common source due to atmospheric conditions.

4. Faulty services: these can be both internal and external services ranging from leaking joints in pipework to fractured drains and rainwater goods.

5. Faulty construction: incorrect assembly and inadequate fixing together with faulty seals are common sources.

6. Poor maintenance: failure to institute or carry out routine maintenance in a cyclic pattern can lead to some of the above-named sources.

7. Incorrect usage: failure to use the fixtures, fittings and services in the correct manner can also lead to failures such as blocked drains and pipes which could then lead to dampness.

Movements

In building movement sources can lead to defects which are small and irritating, such as doors and windows which bind in their frames, but they can also lead to defects which can be very serious such as structural weakness or failure. Movements can be caused by:

1. Soil movements: swelling or shrinking of the soil can have repercussion on the foundations and load-bearing members of the building requiring extensive and costly temporary support measures with permanent underpinning.

2. Temperature movements: buildings are by their nature exposed to the elements and therefore are subject to temperature changes with its resultant expansion and contraction. Buildings should be designed and constructed to accommodate these movements; inadequacy in either could lead to failure. All materials used in movement accommodation suffer deterioration due to age and fatigue and therefore in terms of maintenance they should be inspected and renewed on a regular basis if they are not to become a defect source.

3. Moisture movement: applies to the hygroscopic materials, particularly timber, which must be protected by some form of seal such as paint.

4. Chemical changes: these include corrosion, sulphate attacks and carbonation which can cause disintegration of components, giving rise to movement.

Chemical/biological changes

These changes can be the source of movement and dampness manifestations within buildings and include such sources as corrosion, decay in timber, decomposition of materials due to solar radiation and the incompatibility of materials adjacent to one another.

It is a fundamental mistake when investigating the source of a defect to concentrate on a single source; the true answer is very often to be found in a combination of sources interacting with one another or setting up a chain reaction, and it is the complete tracing of this chain which it is imperative to establish before remedial action is taken. Actual remedial works are not included in this text since the students for whom this book is intended should by now have sufficient technological background to recommend a course of remedial action once the causes and sources have been established. For summary see Fig. 6.8.

Cleaning

The adjective 'clean' can be defined as 'free from anything contaminating or from dirt' and the method of achieving this state is generally termed cleaning. It can be argued that cleaning is not really maintenance since it is work which is not normally undertaken by a building contractor but is usually carried out by a specialist firm or by direct labour. Since the removal of dirt and contaminating agencies from building surfaces can prolong the anticipated useful life of many building materials and components it can therefore be classified as maintenance. The internal and external cleaning costs of many buildings can be over twice as much as the total capital costs and maintenance cost combined throughout the life of the building. There is therefore a need to carefully plan the cleaning aspects of maintenance in line with the statutory provisions and what is desirable.

Cleaning can be carried out for a number of reasons, namely:

1. Aesthetic: this is basically to maintain the appearance of the premises both internally and externally and would range from the daily cleaning of shop windows to complete façade cleaning by specialist contractors. The aesthetic appeal could be to promote or maintain a company's image; it can create the conditions which can lead to a harmonious workforce and thus maximize productivity and it can show up defects at an early stage, thus reducing overall maintenance cost.

2. Health: the removal of dirt will go a long way to removing the breeding ground for many forms of bacteria and discouraging the infestation by rodent and other germ-carrying vermin. The daily cleaning routines of sweeping, washing, dusting and polishing will normally cater for these health aspects and many of these activities are legal requirements, their frequencies being dependent upon the type of premises and occupancy.

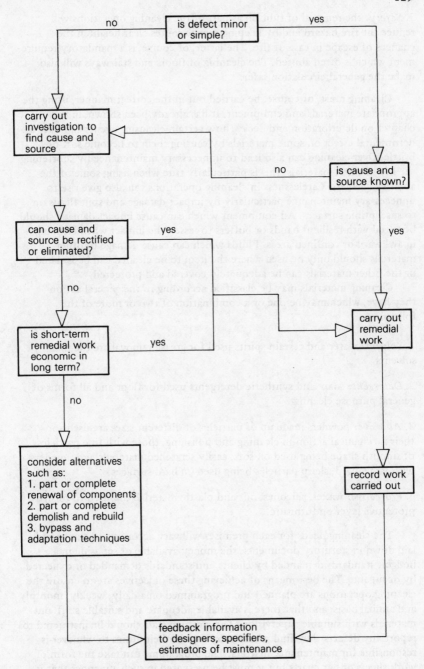

Fig. 6.8. Summary of maintenance decisions

3. Safety: the removal of rubbish as part of the cleaning operations will reduce the fire hazard and by keeping escape routes clear heighten the chances of escape in case of fire. The latter, of course, is a mandatory requirement which is often abused. The cleaning of floors and stairways will also make the general circulation safer.

Cleaning must, of course, be carried out in the correct manner, using the appropriate materials and equipment. It has already been shown, in the chapter on deterioration and decay, how certain cleansing agents can have a detrimental effect on some materials by causing them to become soft or brittle. Over cleaning can also lead to unnecessary maintenance by shortening the life of some materials; this is particularly true when using some of the abrasive cleaners. Carelessness in cleaning operations can also give rise to unnecessary maintenance particularly by impact damage and spilt fluids on to susceptible surfaces. All equipment which can cause impact damage should be fitted with resilient bands or buffers to lessen the impact when cleaning in awkward or confined areas. Fluids which can cause damage to other materials should only be used where the item to be cleaned can be isolated or the other materials can be adequately covered and protected.

Cleaning materials may be classified according to the general action they have, which may be one or a combination of two or more of the following:

1. Solvent: water and certain spirits used for grease removal are the main solvents.

2. Detergent: soap and synthetic detergents used for floor and all forms of general-purpose cleaning.

3. Abrasive: powders made up of particles of different sizes are used for their mechanical action in cleaning and polishing, those with fine particles of smooth shape being used on soft, easily scratched materials and powders with large, hard, sharp particles being used on hard surfaces.

4. Protective: waxes, silicones, oils and plastic materials are used to form a protective layer on furniture.

The cleaning needs for each premises will vary according to the periods laid down in statutory documents, the money available or set aside in a budget, standards demanded by clients and standards demanded or expected by occupants. The best means of achieving these objectives are to ensure the cleaning operations are planned and programmed on a daily, weekly, monthly and annual basis, and that there is available adequate and suitable staff and materials with suitable supervision. The cleaning staff should be instructed to report any defects they find whilst carrying out their duties to whoever is responsible for maintenance matters. The programme can take the form of work sheets or bar charts but it must be presented in such a manner that it is clearly understood by all concerned.

There are many mechanical labour-saving devices such as floor polishers, vacuum machines and applicators which are designed to reduce the labour content, fatigue element and to increase efficiency, but like all items of plant they must be maintained regularly by qualified staff, used as instructed and have a utilization factor which is economic. In the case of large buildings it may be advantageous to employ a cleaning contractor on a regular basis working to an agreed programme.

Quality control and standards

The objective of quality control and standards is to ensure that in an effort to minimize costs the work being carried out is not substandard. The control normally takes the form of periodic inspection of works in progress and of checks and examinations upon completion to ensure that the quality and standard of both materials and workmanship are in keeping with the specification and costs. Work which is being carried out under contract will normally have a clause requiring defects to be made good within a specific time period, but defective work carried out by direct labour has to be made good at the employer's expense. Since both contract and direct labour employed on making good defects will take up extra time, the maintenance work should be planned and undertaken to reduce defects to a minimum. This can be accomplished by the right approach, taking into account the following factors:

1. *Instructions:* these must be clear and concise, setting out exactly what is to be done, when it is to be done, where it is to be done and how it is to be done. Any necessary drawings and specifications should be accurate and clearly indicate the quality and standard required.

2. *Conditions:* the contractor and his staff must be of the right degree of competence and reliable for the work envisaged. He must be given adequate time and access facilities to fulfil the tasks and there must be a degree of flexibility to overcome problems such as adverse weather and unforeseeable snags.

3. *Inspections:* these should be carried out as the situation demands rather than on a regular basis. When the work has reached a difficult or complex stage; before carcassing work is covered in or before services are concealed are ideal times for inspections. If during the inspection variations as to detail, quality or standards are issued, these must be clear and concise, and above all confirmed to avoid any misunderstandings as to their intentions.

Adaptations and extensions

The design procedures described in the foregoing chapters must be applied not only to new buildings but also to adaptations and extensions of existing buildings. In the case of adaptations a feasibility study should be conducted prior to preparing details. This study would not only include economic and design aspects but also the need to obtain any necessary planning permissions or permits. Assuming that the proposed project is feasible and permitted under current legislation, the task of preparing details and specifications can be undertaken.

These documents are a means of communicating to the building contractor what is intended and to this end they must be detailed, clear and unambiguous. Great care must be taken with adaptation work since the work will be carried out within the confines of an existing building or structure which may well have to be altered structurally, therefore both the designer and builder must be aware of the sequence of operations so that any necessary temporary support or protection is in place when required. The design must also conceive the adaptation work in the context of the current Building Regulations which may exclude the use of certain materials or techniques employed in the construction of the existing building.

One of the major concerns of the designer of extension works is joining the proposed extension to the existing structure to form a complete weathertight unit and at the same time achieve an acceptable aesthetic blend. The method of achieving this objective must be clearly shown on the details together with any alterations to the existing structure. Figs. 6.9 to 6.12 show typical details of a simple extension. The chosen example is that of a two-storey extension to an existing dwelling house built in the 1930s and is typical of the many extensions to improve the facilities provided by this kind of property. The details shown in Figs. 6.9 to 6.12 would, in practice, be submitted on one drawing which should be accompanied by a comprehensive specification. The drawing should contain all the necessary information for the submission and approval of planning and Building Regulation requirements and for the setting out and construction on site. Each part of the drawing has a specific use and these are listed below:

1. Small-scale plans (Fig. 6.9): these are the key and block plans which should be drawn to suitable scales; in the case of key plans, not less than 1 : 2500, and for block plans not less than 1 : 1250. The key plan is required for site identification purposes if this is not clear from the block plan, whereas the block plan is required to show:
  i. Size and position of the existing building and the proposed extension.
  ii. Relationship to other buildings and roads.
  iii. Boundaries.
  iv. Drainage layout.

The data for key plans and block plans can be abstracted from ordnance survey maps on payment of a nominal fee. This information is very often obtainable from the local authority building control office.

2. Elevations (Fig. 6.10): these are drawn to small scales such as 1 : 50 and 1 : 20 to show how the existing elevations will be affected by the proposed extension and should give details of matching or contrasting finishes together with details of any opening lights.

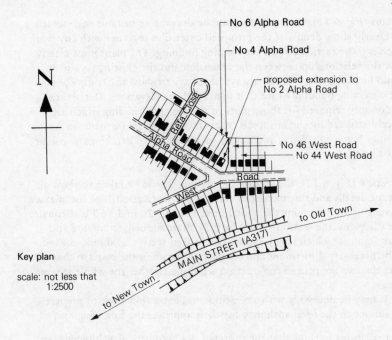

No 6 Alpha Road
No 4 Alpha Road
proposed extension to
No 2 Alpha Road
No 46 West Road
No 44 West Road

Beta Close

Alpha Road

West Road

MAIN STREET (A317)

to Old Town
to New Town

Key plan

scale: not less that
1:2500

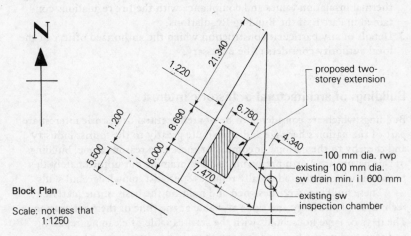

21.340
1.220
8.680
6.000
1.200
5.500
7.470
6.780
4.340

proposed two-
storey extension

100 mm dia. rwp
existing 100 mm dia.
sw drain min. il 600 mm

existing sw
inspection chamber

Block Plan

Scale: not less that
1:1250

Fig. 6.9. Extension example — key and block plans

3. Plans (Fig. 6.11): these plans should be drawn to a suitable scale which will clearly show details of the proposed extension together with any work which is to be carried out on the existing building. The plans must clearly show the relationship between the extension and the existing layout. It should be noted that it is not always necessary to show the complete plan of the existing building or for that matter all the elevations. Details are usually only required for those parts of the existing building which are directly affected by the proposals. A distinction should be made on the drawings between existing and new work by means of hatchings or colour on the prints.

4. Section (Fig. 6.12): the section or sections should be taken to show all relevant details and the maximum amount of information. The complexity will very often determine the scale but usually 1 : 20 or 1 : 50 is adequate. Like the plans, the section should be fully dimensioned, annotated and clearly indicate which is new work. The chosen section(s) should contain all the necessary dimensions and details not shown in the plans so that when the two are read in conjunction with one another the whole scheme is clear.

It may be necessary with alterations and extension work to prepare and submit to the local authority for their approval the following:

1. Calculations to show that the proposal is a permitted development (see Fig. 4.1).
2. Calculations for concrete mix design, structural loadings, structural design, thermal insulation values and compliance with the fire regulations contained in Part E of the Building Regulations.
3. Details of any particular construction which the authorized officer of the local authority considers to be necessary.

Buildings of architectural or historic interest

Buildings which are considered to be of architectural or historic interest are part of the nation's heritage and contribute greatly to the tourist industry and thereby to the national income. For these two reasons alone, buildings of this nature are worth preserving and maintaining but unfortunately this process is very costly and usually requires specialist knowledge and skills.

These buildings were designed and built on the basis of the materials, techniques, knowledge and skills available at the time of their conception. The days of large households with the staff capable of cleaning, repairing and maintaining the building to keep them in good order have largely disappeared due to changes in our society and its structure. The long apprenticeships required to achieve the basic skills of a craft have gone in favour of mass production and prefabricated units and components which require basically fixing skills only. The services of personnel who still have the necessary knowledge and skills are therefore at a premium; likewise the traditional crafts were mainly labour-intensive, which in the light of current

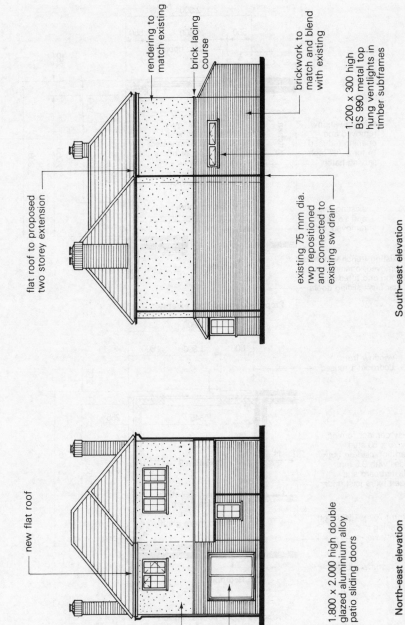

rendering to match existing

brick lacing course

brickwork to match and blend with existing

1.200 x 300 high BS 990 metal top hung ventlights in timber subframes

flat roof to proposed two storey extension

existing 75 mm dia. rwp repositioned and connected to existing sw drain

South-east elevation

new flat roof

proposed two storey extension

1.800 x 2.000 high double glazed aluminium alloy patio sliding doors

North-east elevation

Fig. 6.10. Extension example — elevations

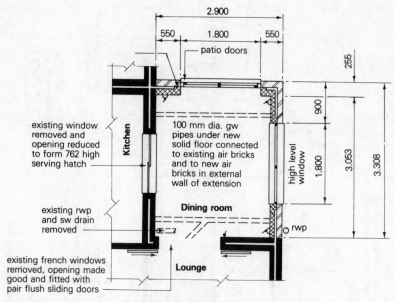

Proposed ground floor extension

2.900

550 1.800 550

patio doors

255

900

high level window

1.800

3.053

3.308

existing window removed and opening reduced to form 762 high serving hatch

Kitchen

100 mm dia. gw pipes under new solid floor connected to existing air bricks and to new air bricks in external wall of extension

Dining room

existing rwp and sw drain removed

rwp

existing french windows removed, opening made good and fitted with pair flush sliding doors

Lounge

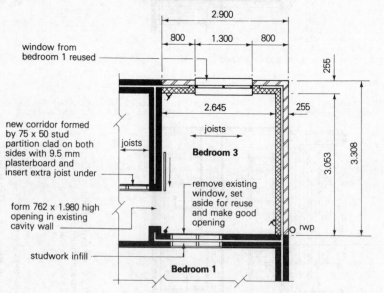

Proposed upper floor extension

2.900

800 1.300 800

window from bedroom 1 reused

255

2.645

255

new corridor formed by 75 x 50 stud partition clad on both sides with 9.5 mm plasterboard and insert extra joist under

joists

joists

Bedroom 3

3.053

3.308

form 762 x 1.980 high opening in existing cavity wall

remove existing window, set aside for reuse and make good opening

rwp

studwork infill

Bedroom 1

Fig. 6.11. Extension example — floor plans

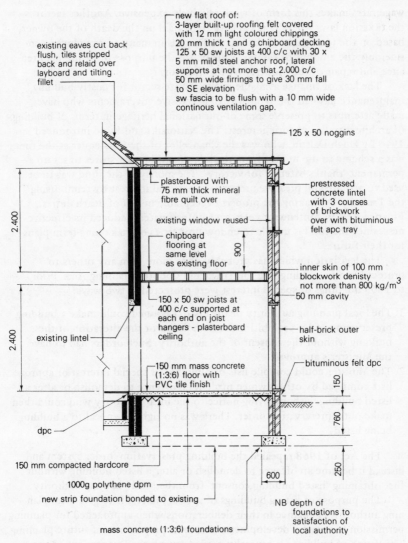

existing eaves cut back flush, tiles stripped back and relaid over layboard and tilting fillet

new flat roof of:
3-layer built-up roofing felt covered with 12 mm light coloured chippings
20 mm thick t and g chipboard decking
125 x 50 sw joists at 400 c/c with 30 x 5 mm mild steel anchor roof, lateral supports at not more that 2.000 c/c
50 mm wide firrings to give 30 mm fall to SE elevation
sw fascia to be flush with a 10 mm wide continous ventilation gap.

125 x 50 noggins

plasterboard with 75 mm thick mineral fibre quilt over

prestressed concrete lintel with 3 courses of brickwork over with bituminous felt apc tray

existing window reused

chipboard flooring at same level as existing floor

900

inner skin of 100 mm blockwork denisty not more than 800 kg/m^3

50 mm cavity

150 x 50 sw joists at 400 c/c supported at each end on joist hangers - plasterboard ceiling

existing lintel

half-brick outer skin

2.400

2.400

150 mm mass concrete (1:3:6) floor with PVC tile finish

bituminous felt dpc

150

dpc

760

150 mm compacted hardcore

1000g polythene dpm

new strip foundation bonded to existing

250

600

mass concrete (1:3:6) foundations

NB depth of foundations to satisfaction of local authority

Fig. 6.12. Extension example — typical section

wage rates makes this form of work relatively expensive. Another factor is the taxation laws whereby taxes have to be paid on the death of the owner, based on the total value of the estate. This has in many cases reduced considerably the amount of capital available for the purpose of future maintenance and repair of the property by its inheritor.

The lack of finance available in the private sector for costly building maintenance has had the sympathy of successive governments who have made attempts to preserve some of our national heritage in terms of buildings of architectural or historic interest. The National Land Fund introduced in 1946 by Hugh Dalton, who was the Chancellor of the Exchequer at the time, was a scheme to use money from the sale of surplus war stores to set up a permanent 'thanks-offering for victory'. The money in the fund was to be used to acquire and preserve property of national interest by reimbursing the Treasury by making the property acceptable in lieu of death duties. Finance Acts in subsequent years have unfortunately reduced its effectiveness, since the fund is unable to endow properties or make long-term plans for their future.

The legislation which has probably done more than any others to protect historic buildings are the Town and Country Planning Acts. Prior to 1969 buildings of special interest were protected in two ways:

1. The local planning authority or the district council could make a building preservation order prohibiting the demolition or the alteration of the building without the consent of the authority. Such orders had to have the Minister's approval.
2. The Minister could compile lists of buildings of special interest or approve lists compiled by others which made it an offence to demolish or alter a listed building without giving notice to the local authority who could then make out a preservation order. There was no right of appeal to a building being listed.

The Act of 1968 repealed the building preservation order system and instead it became an offence to demolish or alter a listed building without first obtaining 'listed building consent' from the local planning authority.

The purpose of listing buildings of special interest is to give local planning authorities guidance in their deliberations when approached for planning permission for nearby developments and in its preparation of future planning. The listing of buildings is generally carried out by the Department of the Environment which lists buildings according to age, architectural value and intrinsic value. Generally all buildings constructed before 1700 which survive in anything like their original condition are listed. Most buildings constructed between 1700 and 1840 are listed on a selective basis. Buildings constructed between 1840 and 1914 are listed if they have a definite quality or character or are the principal work of one of the leading architects of the period.

Under Section 55 of the Act of 1971 it is an offence to carry out, without first obtaining listed building consent, any demolition works, alterations or extensions to a listed building in such a manner which would affect its character as a building of special architectural or historic interest. The procedure for obtaining listed building consent is similar to that described for obtaining planning permission. The Minister must be notified of the intention to grant a consent and he has the power to stop or call in the application. The applicant does, however, have the right of appeal to the Minister whose decision is final unless it can be challenged in High Court proceedings under Section 245 of the Act of 1971. This section enables an application to be made to the High Court on the grounds of the Minister's decision being outside the powers conferred in the Planning Acts or that some procedural requirement of these Acts had not been complied with.

The demolition or alteration of a listed building without consent or in the breaking of any conditions attached to a consent is an offence punishable by fine and/or imprisonment. It is also an offence to demolish a listed building without giving notice to the Royal Commission on Historical Monuments. This is to enable them to inspect and record details of the building before it is demolished. The local planning authority can also serve a 'listed building enforcement notice', specifying the steps to be taken to restore the building to its former state or to secure compliance with the conditions of a listed building consent. The owner or occupier can appeal on certain grounds against a listed building enforcement notice but failure to comply with an enforcement notice is an offence punishable by a fine. The local planning authority may also carry out the work themselves and recover the cost from the owner of the land.

The listing of a building does not impose any obligation on the owner or occupier to the repair of the building but if the building is not kept in a reasonable state of repair the Minister or the local authority may acquire the building by compulsory purchase by following the procedure laid down in the Acquisition of Land (Authorization Procedure) Act 1946. Before such a purchase can be instigated a repairs notice must have been served on the owner at least two months previously. Compensation for the compulsory purchase may be claimed and granted on the basis set out in the Act of 1974 but the amount of compensation payable may be reduced where the building has been deliberately allowed to fall into disrepair for the purposes of justifying its demolition..

The chief sources of revenue for the maintenance of buildings of architectural or historic interest, apart from personal capital, are the grants available upon recommendation of the Historic Buildings Council and grants from the numerous voluntary organizations who devote a great deal of time and effort to the protection and preservation of ancient buildings.

The Historic Buildings Councils were set up under the Historic Building and Ancient Monument Act 1953 to advise the Secretary of State for the Environment as to the allocation of grants for repairs to buildings of outstanding historical or architectural interest. These grants are only available if public access to the property exists in one of four ways:

1. That it is open to the public for a minimum of thirty days each year.
2. That it can be visited by appointment.
3. That the interior, by reason of its use, can be seen by the public.

4. That the exterior is the most important feature and can be seen from the street.

The first two conditions are those which generally affect private properties and the conditions imposed may well deter the owner from making an application for a grant, since if the public are to be admitted provision for toilets and car parking would have to be made. The cost of providing these facilities would have to be borne by the owner since the grant would only cover repair costs.

It can be seen from the above comments that the preservation, maintenance and adaptation of buildings of special, architectural or historic interest requires careful consideration in terms of legal obligations, availability of grants towards the costs involved and the scarcity of suitable and experienced staff to design, plan and carry out the necessary works. Government attitudes to this problem are constantly changing both in concept and as to the amount of money being made available. It is therefore necessary to be well advised as to these aspects before contemplating or undertaking work of this nature.

Chapter 7

Maintenance management

Management can be defined in general terms as the task of seeing that a job gets done and is carried out efficiently. This is true of whatever enterprise or activity is being undertaken. Within the overall definition given above the basic facets of management can be listed thus:

1. *Planning*: this would include organizing the department or firm, ensuring that all the necessary items such as equipment, tools, materials, work instructions and adequate labour are available at the required time. Another aspect would be the setting of targets for expected outcome and performance to ensure viability or profitability.

2. *Controlling*: this is the continuous process of checking actual performance against planned performance and making any necessary alterations to ensure a satisfactory performance and outcome is achieved. It should also include the recording and feeding back of information gained by experience for the benefit of future planning.

3. *Co-ordinating*: this is the balancing and keeping of the team together as a harmonious unit by suitable and fair allocation of work.

4. *Motivating*: this is the management role of leadership involving inspiring loyalty, effectiveness, pride and a sense of moral responsibility to the tasks set within a team or group so that an effective and economic outcome is assured.

Organization structure

Maintenance activities can be carried out by labour employed directly by the company or owner of a premises or alternatively by an outside contractor employing his own labour force. In preparing an organization structure the initial decision must be taken as to whether direct or contract labour will be employed. If the decision to use a combination of direct and contract workers is made then the balance or ratio between them must be established.

The actual structure of a maintenance department will be governed by several factors such as the size of the firm, the anticipated work load, budget or money allocation and the overall policy towards employing direct labour. In large companies the employment of direct labour to cover the major fields of maintenance such as cleaning, services and decorations is usually considered necessary, whereas in smaller firms it may be possible to allocate some of the maintenance tasks as part of or in addition to other tasks or duties.

The functions of a maintenance department must also be taken into account when preparing the organization structure and these would include:

1. Organizational function: this would include work allocation, paths of responsibility and accountability, setting standards and procedures, establishing lines of communication, providing the necessary accommodation and equipment, employing staff, purchasing materials and preparing and administrating contracts where outside contractors are engaged.

2. Control and planning function: this would include inspecting and reporting on the need for maintenance works to be carried out, planning and programming of the works both in the short and long term contexts, preparing costing and budgetary statements, controlling quality and quantity of output by establishing an adequate supervisory system and organizing a system of recording and feeding back information for future use in planning.

3. Advisory function: this would include informing and advising management on maintenance policy, standards, cost requirements and giving advice as to the maintenance aspects at the design stage of any proposed new buildings, extensions or adaptations.

Other aspects which could come under the jurisdiction of a maintenance department are fire precautions and safety, general security and safety measures and possibly the collection and disposal of waste and refuse.

Contract and direct labour

Before any decision can be taken as to whether a company is best served by a contract or direct labour force for maintenance work the advantages and disadvantages of the alternatives should be considered, bearing in mind that within any maintenance organization occasions will arise when it is necessary and/or desirable to employ a specialist firm from outside the organization.

Advantages of a direct labour force

1. Flexibility: full control over the movement and work allocation of a direct labour force will give greater flexibility and quicker response to any emergency which may arise. If production is held up or reduced due to lack of maintenance the loss to a company in terms of production and goodwill can be considerable. Control over a direct force can also go a long way to limiting the need for emergency maintenance by being able to establish and supervise a system of regular planned and preventive maintenance.

2. Intimate knowledge: the members of a direct labour force acquire over a period of time an intimate knowledge of the building, its services and equipment which has to be maintained. This can be a great asset where there is a large volume of services and equipment, since, although the services and items of equipment may well be standard components, they can develop their own peculiarities; familiarity with these can very often speed up the diagnosis of the fault and the remedy required to put the equipment or service back into operation with the minimum of delay. This will help promote good relationships between the users and the maintenance staff.

3. Control: a direct labour system enables management to control more effectively the overall strategy of maintenance work since the staff and their individual abilities and limitations will be known; similarly the balance of the labour as to whether it should be of a craft or engineering bias in view of the maintenance problems which could occur. The planning of the work load should also be under better control with a direct labour force rather than contract labour, as set out above under 1 (Flexibility). The quality control should also be superior since directly employed maintenance staff can be motivated into doing an effective job because any future maintenance caused by inadequate workmanship will have to be corrected by themselves.

Disadvantages of a direct labour force

It is very difficult to be specific on the disadvantages of a direct labour force since each type of premises and/or company has different problems. In small companies the workforce could well be underemployed; insufficient planned or preventive maintenance to keep them fully occupied may lead to the staff waiting for something to go wrong. In large companies it may be necessary to call in outside contractors to ease the work load. This is particularly true with regard to buildings such as large schools where redecorations would be confined to vacation periods, thus putting an impossible task on to the direct labour maintenance staff who are generally responsible for the day-to-day maintenance activities.

It can also be argued that a large direct labour force is very often better equipped to deal with problems which occur within their jurisdiction, but they do not always have within the force the necessary qualified or experienced staff to take full advantage of the facilities provided. Productivity is often quoted as being higher with contract maintenance workers since many of the personnel employed on direct labour teams are older, having opted for a steady, secure job without the pressures of contract work coupled with incentive bonus schemes based on quantity rather than quality. The counter argument is that the older employee tends to have greater knowledge and skills than his younger counterpart and this reduces the overall amount of maintenance required. No really convincing statistics are available to justify either argument.

The main disadvantage tends therefore to be in the productivity of a direct labour maintenance department which can be as low as 65 per cent, not necessarily due to poor workmanship or lack of work but very often by its nature and location. Local authority housing is a typical example; many of the maintenance tasks are not within themselves time consuming but travelling between the premises to carry out these small jobs can result in a large proportion of non-productive work time. Would contract workers in this instance be any cheaper? This is a question to which there cannot be a direct answer since it would depend on the type of arrangement or contract. If contract labour is employed to carry out small isolated works over a large area it could well be more expensive than direct labour, even allowing for low productivity, but if the maintenance contract is on a long-term basis whereby the contractor is called upon to supply the necessary labour and materials as required a saving could well be made, since only productive time would be chargeable. This form of contract enables the contractor to direct his labour force on to other work when the maintenance requirements are low or non-existent.

If any conclusion is to be made as to whether direct or contract labour is to be used for maintenance work it must be based on the work load available and the amount of unproductive time anticipated caused by such items as travelling between jobs. Maintenance has now begun to be taken so seriously by many management teams that it seems in future a more reliable answer to the choice of labour force will be able to be found by examining feedback information and costings. It will in most instances, however, remain a balance between the two options and achieving the correct balance must be one of the aims of management.

Communications needs

If a satisfactory design is to be evolved in terms of capital expenditure, user requirements, running and maintenance costs, the designer will need specific information during the various design stages which must be communicated to the designer in a manner which is unambiguous, so that by using the information the desired result can be achieved. The design stages or steps have already been discussed in Chapter 2 and summarized in Fig. 2.1. The information required at each stage can be listed as follows:

1. *Initial brief:* the designer will require at this stage an outline of the requirements and objectives proposed for the new building, extension or adaptation. This would consist of the basic site particulars, approximate areas for the various usages together with population densities, service requirements,

standards required and any time and cost targets. This information should enable the designer to produce sketch designs and approximate cost summaries.

2. Working drawings and specification: the sketch designs and approximate costings should have been approved and specific information will now be required to enable the working drawings and specification to be prepared. It is at this stage that the detailed information should be supplied with regards to all aspects of the project and in particular the provisions for maintenance. The latter would include any special features required in terms of access to parts of the building or its equipment in the context of the maintenance policy of the building owner. Any restrictions as to choice of materials based on the proposed methods of cleaning or renewal should be communicated, especially in the context of floors (which forms probably the biggest maintenance, cleaning and safety problem in any building). The layout and loading of services to give the requirements at specific points needs to be communicated along with any restrictions as to the flexibility and working space in the context of future changes and modifications which may be necessary, since the poor location and layout of such permanent elements as ducts, stairs and lifts can very often determine what future changes in layout can or cannot be undertaken.

The above information can be communicated to the designer in the form of detailed written instructions, sketch drawings of any specific requirements and manufacturers' detailed literature for special materials, equipment or fixtures. For a very detailed brief the basic information can be conveyed to the designer by means of a form or table setting out the design requirements on a room-by-room basis which would identify the room, its use, population density and give requirements as to construction method, finishes, fittings and services for walls, floors, ceilings, doors, windows and any other items.

3. Choice of contractor: the method of selecting a contractor will very often depend upon the size and nature of the work to be undertaken. Simple and relatively small buildings on clear isolated sites are usually straightforward contracts for which full documentation is available and are therefore suitable for a fixed price tender obtained by competition from a selected number of contractors. Large buildings and congested sites are, however, best served by competitive tenders from selected contractors probably based on a Bill of Approximate Quantities. This would enable an early start to be made whilst the detailed working drawings and specification are being prepared or completed.

Alteration work, particularly if it is complicated, is very often better if based on a negotiated price with a contractor specializing in the type of work. In many cases it is even better to contract on a cost plus basis; that is, the cost of the actual labour and materials used plus an agreed percentage to cover overheads and profit – since a tender figure would have to include a generous allowance for items whereby the true extent and nature of work involved is not certain until work actually starts on site.

The above decisions and methods of communication must come from management and they will in turn need guidance, advice and information from the various sections under their control. This can result from discussions and from any feedback information available. Projected trends must also be taken into account so that the maximum amount of flexibility of the proposed building or adaptation can be obtained not only upon completion but also in the future. In this context the maintenance policy of the management is very important since the successful running and maintenance of any building will only be possible if it can be carried out in a satisfactory manner; for this objective to be economically achieved short- and long-term maintenance must be planned and incorporated in the design.

Health and safety responsibilities

There are many Acts of Parliament which set out the legal obligations of management as to their responsibilities with regard to the health and safety of their workforces and workplaces, all of which now come under the umbrella of the enabling Act entitled The Health and Safety at Work, etc., Act 1974. This Act, which is in addition to and only partially replacing existing health and safety laws and regulations has already been defined in general terms in Chapter 4 dealing with legislation. Although the greater part of existing Acts and the Statutory Instruments made under them remain in force until amended or repealed by this Act it does extend the scope of health and safety legislation since it applies to all persons at work including employers, employees and self-employed persons with the exception of domestic servants in private households. This Act also ensures that the health and safety legislation protects not only people at work but also the general public who may be affected by any work activities.

Part I of this Act relates to health and safety and sets out in Section 2 the duties of the employer, which are to:

(a) provide and maintain plant in a safe condition without any risks to health;
(b) arrange for the safe handling, storage and transportation of goods;
(c) as far as reasonably practicable make any place of work under his control safe and to maintain its safe condition without risks to health;
(d) ensure that the means of access and egress from a workplace are maintained in a safe condition without risks to health;
(e) provide and maintain a safe and healthy environment in which to work;
(f) provide and maintain good welfare facilities;
(g) provide instruction, training and supervision of persons so that their health and safety is safeguarded;
(h) set standards to safeguard the well-being of all employees.

Section 2(3) of this Act also instructs all employers to prepare, and as often as may be appropriate revise, a written policy statement with respect to the health and safety at work of his employees and its organization, which should include the arrangements for ensuring that the stated policy is carried out. A typical statement would include a general description of the objectives under headings such as:

1. Maintenance of plant, equipment and safe systems of work.
2. Safe arrangements for the use, handling, storage and transport of articles, materials and substances.
3. Information, instruction, training and supervision to enable all employees to contribute positively to their own and others' safety and health at work and to avoid hazards.
4. Provision and maintenance of safety equipment and protective clothing and ensuring that all employees are informed of their obligations with regard to care and use.
5. A safe and healthy place of work and safe access and egress from it for employees and members of the public.
6. Adequate welfare facilities.

Other sections of the written statement would include the policy objectives as to:

(*a*) safety organization;
(*b*) employees' responsibilities;
(*c*) safe operating procedures of equipment, plant and apparatus;
(*d*) accident procedures;
(*e*) fire procedures;
(*f*) inspections and checks;
(*g*) training;
(*h*) means of communication.

Safety representatives

Sections 2.4 and 2.5 of the Health and Safety at Work, etc, Act require consultation between employer and employee to ensure the health and safety of workers and to check on the effectiveness of the arrangements made. The employees' legally appointed representative's main task is to represent a particular group of employees. Under this Act the safety representative could be appointed by either:

1. Election from among employees.
2. Appointment by independent recognized trade unions.

Subsequent legislation in the form of the Employment Protection Act 1975 removed the election from among employees and now the only legal way an employee may be appointed as a safety representative is as a nominee of an independent recognized trade union which is defined in the Employment Protection (Consolidation) Act 1978 as one which is:

(*a*) not under the domination or control of an employer or group of employers or of one or more employers' association;
(*b*) not liable to interference by an employer or any such group or association tending towards such control.

An independent trade union as defined above becomes recognized when an employer recognizes it for the purpose of negotiation.

A safety representative has considerable powers with regard to the right to investigate hazards, complaints, carry out inspections, make representations to employers, receive information from inspectors and attend safety committee meetings. A safety representative's duties and rights together with those of the safety committee are set out in the Statutory Instrument, entitled the Safety Representatives and Safety Committee Regulations 1977 which came into force on 1 October 1978.

Part II of the Health and Safety at Work, etc, Act sets out the functions of and responsibility for maintaining an Employment Medical Advisory Service whose duties are basically to advise persons who are employed, seeking or training for employment on matters safeguarding and improving the health of such persons. An employment medical adviser must be a fully registered medical practitioner. This part does not completely supersede the Employment Medical Advisory Service Act 1972 but basically re-enacts the provisions contained therein with amendments.

Part III of the Health and Safety at Work, etc, Act gives provisions to extend the scope and coverage of the Building Regulations by amending the provisions contained in the Public Health Acts of 1936 and 1961 regarding building regulations. Provisions can now be made to include regulations to conserve fuel, power and water. It also allows regulations to be made which would impose a continuous requirement on owners and occupiers with regard to the maintenance of services, fittings and equipment whether or not the building under consideration was constructed under the current Building Regulations. It also allows conditions to be imposed regarding the use and inspection of services, fittings and equipment and also regarding the use or continuation of use of short-lived materials.

From the above brief comments regarding this Act it can be seen that its powers and repercussions can be very wide and therefore management must keep themselves well informed of the changes as they occur if a successful maintenance policy is to be conceived and carried out.

Property inspections and reports

Buildings and their contents may be inspected for a number of reasons and the purpose of such an inspection must be established before commencement if a satisfactory report should be agreed so that all the necessary information is obtained and recorded in an acceptable manner. The report form should be designed to ensure that as far as practicable there are no omissions. The types of inspection that can be carried out may be listed thus:

1. Complete building inspection or survey.
2. Inspect and rectify.
3. Planned inspections.
4. Control inspections.

Complete building inspection or survey

This form of inspection is usually carried out to obtain a complete and accurate record of the property, its services and fixtures and would normally be carried out where such data does not exist, particularly at the beginning of a lease or prior to purchase. The inspection or survey needs to be carried out by an experienced surveyor, and in the case of older buildings one who has a good knowledge of that type or era of construction. The information should be gathered in such a manner that when finally presented, errors and omissions have been reduced to a minimum.

The building should be measured with a tape and using 'running dimensions' to reduce the risk of cumulative errors which can easily occur when measuring 'piecemeal'. All fittings, fixtures, services and any other features must be noted and measured to obtain their position and size. To ensure accuracy when plotting or preparing the scaled drawings, check dimensions in the form of diagonals and offsets should be taken. It is essential that sufficient information and dimensions should be collected and recorded on site by means of sketch plans, elevations and sections to enable a set of scaled drawings to be made. It is also worth considering taking a series of external and internal photographs to supplement the scaled drawings; usually black and white photographs will show more detail and have better definition than colour prints. A written report should also be prepared as to the condition, want of repair or any other items in need of attention and this report should be submitted with the drawings. The drawings may be presented in the form of fully dimensioned and annotated working drawings or, alternatively, as measured drawings without dimensions or annotation but including a drawn scale. For typical examples of property inspection or survey sketches see Figs. 7.1 and 7.2

Inspect and rectify

This form of inspection can usually be carried out by a competent operative. The inspection may well be planned as to timing or carried out as the result of a request from the user. Typical examples are the inspection of and cleaning out as necessary rainwater gutters and downpipes, and the checking and adjustment of self-closing door springs. A report of the inspection and any action taken should be submitted for record purposes or alternatively this information could be extracted from timesheets or works order sheets.

Planned inspections

Buildings can be simple or complex, domestic or commercial and therefore it is essential with any form of planned inspection to define exactly the purpose of the inspection and the competence or qualifications of the inspector or surveyor. As far as practicable a survey sheet should be designed and used to enable the inspector or surveyor to record his findings, and therefore the survey sheet should be so formulated to avoid the possibility of items being overlooked or omitted. A typical example of such a survey sheet is shown in Fig. 7.3.

Planned inspections can be undertaken for a number of reasons such as:

1. To prepare a complete inventory or record of the premises as to its condition and contents in the form of services, fittings and fixtures.

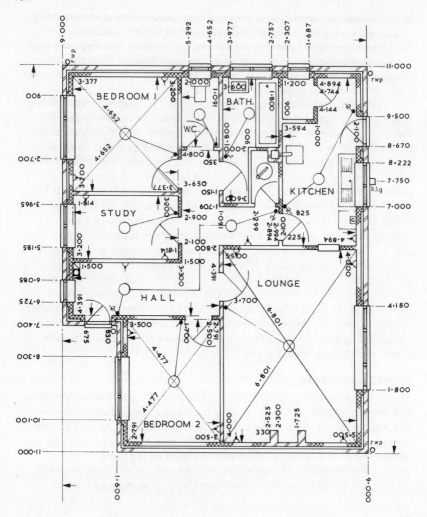

NB This plan to be read in conjunction with the
section shown in Fig. 7.2.

Fig. 7.1. Typical site inspection or survey sketch plan

2. To ascertain the need for any current, predicted or future maintenance for the purposes of planning the workload and/or the budget.
3. To investigate the cause and extent of any occurrence necessitating maintenance so that its priority can be determined and also the standard of maintenance required.

For planned inspections the need for recording the information and data obtained and using this in a feedback system cannot be over emphasized. The system used to store the information and data should ensure that easy retrieval is possible and such a filing system could range from one based on location, item or service, inspection date, to one based on a trade or craft classification. Any or all of these headings could be used but if more than one is selected there should be an adequate system of cross referencing. Card index systems are probably better than box or lever arch filing systems for both storage and easy retrieval.

Control inspections

This form of inspection is to check that any maintenance work carried out has been executed in a workmanlike manner in accordance with the instructions issued and that it is up to the standard required by the firm's maintenance policy. By carrying out such inspections as a matter of routine a measure of control can be obtained over the quality and quantity of maintenance work undertaken.

From the moment any property inspection is planned or requested by the user, a chain of events should be followed to ensure that a successful conclusion is reached and that the whole process is recorded for historical record and feedback purposes. For a summary of planned inspections see Fig. 7.4.

Estimates for maintenance and adaptation works

Before management issues instructions to carry out maintenance or adaptation work an estimate of the likely costs and time should be evaluated so that cash needs, labour force required and priorities can be established. Management may require this information for any of the following reasons:

1. To enable comparisons to be made between competitive estimates obtained from outside contractors.
2. To establish long- and short-term budget requirements.
3. To apportion or allocate moneys from an existing budget.
4. To provide evidence for a request for extra moneys where necessary maintenance or adaptation is not included or covered by an existing budget.

To enable an estimate to be formulated the estimator will require both data and an agreed system by which an estimated figure may be calculated.

The data available will govern the accuracy which can be achieved by the estimator in preparing his figures and he will require information on:

152

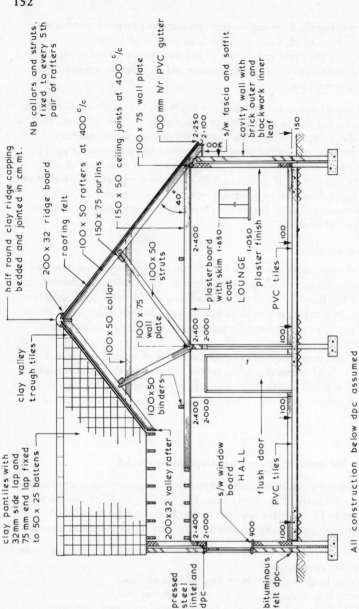

clay pantiles with
32mm side lap and
75 mm end lap fixed
to 50 x 25 battens

clay valley trough tiles

200 x 32 valley rafter

pressed steel lintel and dpc

bituminous felt dpc

half round clay ridge capping bedded and jointed in cm. mt.

NB collars and struts. fixed to every 5th pair of rafters

200 x 32 ridge board

roofing felt

100 x 50 collar

100 x 75 wall plate

100 x 50 struts

100 x 50 binders

s/w window board

HALL

flush door

PVC tiles

100 x 50 rafters at 400 °/c

150 x 75 purlins

100 x 50 ceiling joists at 400 °/c

100 x 75 wall plate

100 mm h/r PVC gutter

s/w fascia and soffit

cavity wall with brick outer and blockwork inner leaf

plasterboard with skim coat

LOUNGE

PVC tiles

40°

1·650

1·050 plaster finish

2·250
2·100

300

2·400
2·000

2·400
2·000

2·400
2·000

2·400
2·000

150

100

100

100

100

900

All construction below dpc assumed

NB This section is to be read in conjunction with the plan shown in Fig. 7.1

Fig. 7.2. Typical site inspection or survey sketch section

survey sheet 1 of 13

location   LOUNGE

4 West Avenue
New Town
Surrey

Survey taken 23 November 1979 - house unoccupied

Ceilings: plaster finish coated with emulsion paint - slight cracking to perimeter around chimney - no pattern staining

Walls: plaster finish 3 walls papered 1 wall emulsion paint finish 100 mm high pencil round softwood painted skirting m/c 12%

Floors: PVC grey mottled tiles   4 No. 225 x 225 tiles loose – location near to hearth

Windows: 4 light softwood painted glazed with clear glass   internal sill painted softwood 200 mm wide m/c 11%

Doors: plywood flush size 1.98 x 762 painted - BMA latch   architrave 75 x 20 softwood splayed pattern painted

Fittings: cast stone fireplace surround with green polished slate mantle and hearth - minor smoke staining to stonework over fire recess - fireback badly cracked, needs replacing - fret satisfactory

Decorations: generally in poor condition throughout – complete redecoration required

Plumbing: nil

Electric: plastic ceiling rose and pendant bayonet fixing with 400 mm drop - flex to be renewed - 5 No ring main outlets

Gas: Nil

Heating: open fire only - see comments under fittings

Fig. 7.3. Typical survey sheet

1. Nature of proposed work.
2. Extent or scope of work.
3. Method of operation.
4. Restrictions of any kind.
5. Current labour costs and availability.
6. Current material costs and availability.
7. Data on past performances for the same or similar tasks and conditions, usually obtained from feedback information or historical records.
8. Direct or contract labour considerations.
9. Specialist services and/or fees.

The estimate itself can be detailed or approximate depending on the purpose for which it is required.

Rough or approximate estimates are a quick and simple method of assessing likely costs and should be based on past records and performances which need to be adjusted to take into account any current inflation trends, or, if formulating costs for budget purposes, any predicted or projected trends. Adjustments may also have to be made for any variations in the condition or nature of the work with regard to the recorded data being used. The systems which can be employed for this type of estimating are:

1. Cost per floor area: this can be based on the square metre or, for large areas, on 100 square metres. Different uses of floor areas can give different costs for similar tasks. The floor area is usually measured gross inside the external walls.

2. Cost per volume: this method is basically an alternative to the above method and is normally employed when considering large units of accommodation such as factories and hospitals. The volume is usually measured gross over the external walls.

3. Cost per accommodation: the unit on which this method is based is the number of persons using the premises and is useful as an overall measure of maintenance costs for buildings of similar age, use and construction such as schools, hotels and hospitals.

4. Cost per element: this method can be more accurate than the above-mentioned systems since the costs are calculated by each element involved and these are related to an overall classification such as the total floor area. The breakdown into the number of elements to be considered governs the overall accuracy. Elements such as floors, walls, ceilings, windows and doors are typical components of the estimate. Areas such as floors and walls would be considered on a square metre basis, whereas doors and windows could alternatively be enumerated.

Where past data or records do not exist, guidance as to cost comparisons can be obtained from the Building Maintenance Cost Information Service (BMCIS) which was established and sponsored by the Department of the Environment and the Royal Institution of Chartered Surveyors in 1970.

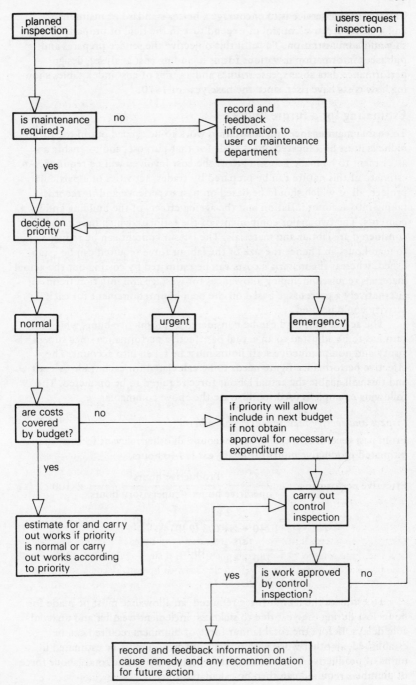

Fig. 7.4. Summary of planned inspections

The aim of this service is to encourage a better standard of maintenance and a more effective control of expenditure in the field of property ownership and administration. To fulfil this objective the service prepares and publishes information in various forms including cost analyses, design/ performance data sheets, case studies and a series of cost index tables showing how costs have risen since the base year of 1970.

Estimating for a future budget

To enable maintenance and adaptation work to be carried out in the future, moneys must be allocated or set aside for that purpose, and to enable an assessment to be made an estimate of the cost involved will be required. An estimate of this nature can be prepared by trades, activities or a particular project, all of which should be based on past experience and/or records, taking into account inflation and the ageing effects of the building and its contents. The two major components of the estimate which have to be considered are labour and materials. The labour content can be reduced to man-hours and hence the size of the labour force required can be established, whereas the materials costs can be estimated by costing out the actual materials required including allowances for wastage and inflation trends or alternatively a percentage based on the man-hour requirement for each activity could be used.

The actual workload can be considered as productive hours which in turn has to be adjusted to an actual or effective performance since supervisory and non-productive staff hours must be taken into account. The effective performance figure needs to be calculated for each trade or craft and this will enable the actual labour force required to be predicted. The following example is used to illustrate the above comments:

Inspect and rectify maintenance – plumbers

From past records and taking into account all other relevant factors, the estimated productive hours for next year is 240 hours.

$$\text{Effective performance} = \frac{\text{Productive hours}}{\text{operative hours} + \text{supervisory hours}} \times 100$$

$$= \frac{240}{240 + \text{say } 0.2\,(240)} \times 100$$

$$= \frac{240}{240 + 48} \times 100$$

$$= 83.3$$

To estimate the labour force required, an allowance must be made for hours lost during the year due to sickness, inclement weather and unavoidable delays. Before the total labour force of plumbers required can be established, all other work within their jurisdiction must be estimated in terms of productive hours and effective performance. The total labour force of plumbers required can then be calculated thus:

$$\text{Total labour force} = \frac{(TPH \times \frac{100}{EP}) + LTA \ (TPH \times \frac{100}{EP})}{HPY}$$

where TPH = total productive hours obtained by adding together the predicted productive hours for each activity (say 14 000).

          EP = effective performance (say 83.3)

         LTA = lost time allowance (say 15%)

        HPY = hours per year per man

             = 40 hours per week × 46 weeks (allowing for annual holidays and public holidays)

             = 1840 hours

$$\text{therefore labour force} = \frac{(14\,000 \times \frac{100}{83.3}) + \frac{15}{100} (14\,000 \times \frac{100}{83.3})}{1840}$$

$$= \frac{(16\,806.72) + 0.15\,(16\,806.72)}{1840}$$

$$= \frac{16\,806.72 + 2521}{1840}$$

$$= 10.5$$

Say 11 men

For individual activities a similar calculation can be made to obtain the gang size required:

Gang size required for inspect and rectify maintenance by plumbers

$$= \frac{(TPH \times \frac{100}{EP}) + LTA \ (TPH \times \frac{100}{EP})}{TA}$$

where TA = time allowed (say 2 weeks = 80 hours)

$$\text{therefore gang size} = \frac{(240 \times \frac{100}{83.3}) + 0.15 (240 \times \frac{100}{83.3})}{80}$$

$$= \frac{(288.12) + 0.15\,(288.12)}{80}$$

$$= \frac{288.12 + 43.22}{80}$$

$$= 4.14$$

Say 4 men.

Having established that a total labour force of eleven plumbers would be required to carry out the predicted work load the budget sum to be requested can be calculated by taking into account the following costs:

1. All-in wage rates of labour force – this would include basic wages plus bonus or other payments such as profit-sharing payments together with all employer's statutory payments and contributions.
2. Estimated material costs.
3. Establishment and overhead charges.
4. Any element of profit required.
5. All-in costs to cover supervisory and other non-productive staff.

Other estimates may also be required to cover any proposed contract or tendered work to be included in the future budget. The actual contract or tender figure will be calculated by the contractor's own staff using the traditional methods based on a bill of quantities, specification and/or drawings by computing unit rates for each item and collecting these to give a final total to which can be added sums to cover overheads and profit. However, to enable a sum to be included in a future budget for maintenance, an estimate should be prepared by using any of the rough or approximate estimating techniques described above or by calculating unit rates in the same manner as an outside contractor. The object of this exercise is in fact twofold. First, it is used to obtain a figure for inclusion in the budget, and second, it can be used as a comparative figure when considering the actual tender sums received from outside contractors.

Estimating within a current budget

Moneys may have been allocated in a current budget for a specific item or activity such as the redecoration of the façade and therefore no estimate would be required to obtain an allocation of money from the current budget. Upon completion the job should be costed so that the actual cost can be compared with the predicted or estimated cost used to prepare the budget and the information so obtained from the exercise used in feedback information for preparing future estimates. Moneys may also have been allocated in the current budget for use in a particular field or by a specific craft or trade without actually being allocated to a particular task. An estimate of how much money should be expended on any of these tasks could be prepared and this would enable a certain amount of control to be exercised over current budget moneys allocation for unspecified maintenance work.

The actual method of calculation will depend on the nature of the task and can range from spot item pricing to a unit rate pricing system against actual quantities of labour and material requirements. The same processes can be applied when requesting extra finance over and above the current budget allocation except that the reasons and costs would probably have to be very detailed to convince management that such extra expense is both necessary and justifiable.

Estimating is very often referred to as 'guesstimating', and indeed to a certain extent this is true, but if management is going to provide the

necessary finance it must have definite guidelines as to what maintenance
and adaptation will be necessary and how much it is going to cost. Accuracy
in this field can only be obtained if the data and information used in the
preparation of estimates is in itself accurate and that future trends, particularly in the context of inflation, have been taken into account.

Specifications for maintenance and adaptation works

A specification may be defined as a written document setting out in detail
the exact nature and contents of the work, the minimum standard of
workmanship which is acceptable together with the materials to be used.
This document needs to be written and read in conjunction with any drawings, schedules and bills of quantities produced to cover the proposed works.
A specification may be either concise or lengthy according to the amount
of information contained in the other contract documents. A specification
should not supersede the particulars or information given in other documents
but should clarify or amplify the information where it is not clearly given or
can be subject to misinterpretation.

Drawings usually show the general arrangement and details of the
proposed works and the specification should describe the exact requirements
of these details and arrangements. All the important dimensions and annotation should be included on the drawings and therefore it is not usually
necessary to include in the specification the general dimensions such as room
sizes but the sizes of individual members such as joists and rafters should
always be quoted. On small works where drawings or details are not provided
the specification must fully describe the works and include all relevant
information and dimensions. A specification which is detailed, but at the
same time concise, will help to prevent mistakes and misunderstandings during
the preparation period and whilst the works are in progress.

A specification can be prepared by the designer, a quantity surveyor or,
where the works are small and no designer is involved by the client, maintenance manager or building contractor. The preparation in all circumstances
should, however, follow the same pattern of drafting, checking, amending
as necessary, producing a final draft, checking, making a fair copy and,
before issue, the final check. This process may seem to be laborious, but
since a specification can be a legal contract document it will be followed only
as far as it goes; therefore, a full, accurate, detailed and unambiguous specification is required if conflicts and disputes are to be avoided.

Generalizations in a specification such as 'as required' and 'as necessary'
should be avoided since they are open to different interpretations and give
the impression that the person preparing the specification is not sure of what
is required or what the consequences of any action will be. It is also unfair
to expect an estimator to give an accurate price on a vague statement and
this in turn could lead to claims for extra payment when the time comes
for presenting and settling the final account. If the person preparing the
specification is not sure of the proper description, the exact nature of the

work or what will actually be required on site, a provisional sum should be included which can then be adjusted by agreement between the parties concerned when settling the final account. It follows therefore that as far as possible all descriptions and clauses contained in a specification should be definite, clear and comprehensive.

Preparation and contents of a specification

The actual preparation and format of a specification will be governed by three factors:

1. Who is to carry out the preparation?
2. What is its purpose?
3. Who will use it?

If the preparation is to be carried out by an owner or occupier for the purpose of internal instruction or to obtain an estimate it is most likely to be non-technical in its content and grouped in areas of activity such as repairs to a roof. The descriptions would probably be all embracing; that is, not separated into materials and labour or classified by trades and without any indication of quality for materials and workmanship. As an internal document it is usually satisfactory since the maintenance manager or worker would be familiar with this form of presentation and could analyse the document in a suitable manner for estimating, costing, ordering and job instruction purposes; but if this type of specification is used as a basis for obtaining an estimate from an outside building contractor it could lead to ambiguities and misunderstandings of both the content and intent of the descriptions or clauses. This in turn could lead to an estimate which is unreal and ultimately to claims from the contractor for remeasurement or extra costs. If estimates are to be sought from several contractors the weakness of this form of specification can be even more pronounced than when negotiating with a single contractor. It follows therefore that whenever possible a specification should be prepared by a person who has the necessary technical knowledge to set out the requirements in a clear and understandable manner.

Specifications prepared by a designer or quantity surveyor usually follow a definite pattern such as work areas, trade sections or activity sections as set out in the Standard Method of Measurement of Building Works, but usually all correctly prepared specifications commence with clauses covering:

1. Preliminaries.
2. Materials.
3. Workmanship.
4. General clauses.

These clauses would be followed by specific requirements as to the works in particular or the works in general.

1. Preliminaries: these clauses would include information regarding the site, possession or starting date, brief description of the works to be executed, any drawings to be used in conjunction with the specification, general contract conditions and responsibilities for insurance, protection of existing works, hoardings and general storage facilities.

2. *Materials:* clauses should give a general description of the materials to be used stating the standard or quality required by reference to a particular document such as a British Standard, Code of Practice or an Agrément Certificate. If such a document does not exist for a particular material or component a full description should be given devoid of all vague terms such as 'best available', 'suitable' and 'good quality', which are all liable to different interpretations. To save unnecessary repetition, materials and components which are to be used for several activities could be fully described at this juncture instead of repeating the description every time the item appears in the specification.

3. *Workmanship:* as with materials, the requirements should be precise, setting out in detail the manner in which the work is to be executed in terms of quality and method. Allowances or restrictions for such items as inclement weather and the use of alternative methods should also be stated. References to any relevant British Standard or Code of Practice should also be included so as to clarify the minimum standards acceptable.

4. *General clauses:* with new works it is traditional to prepare a specification in the same order and groupings as for taking off a bill of quantities but maintenance work which is small or isolated in content is very often written to cover an area of activity, thus enabling the contractor the opportunity of seeing at a glance the extent of the work so that a fair and accurate estimate can be given. A typical example of such a description is given below to illustrate this point.

Roofwork: strip off and remove existing roof slates, slate battens and roofing felt and remove all nails over a single area of approximately 9 m^2. Supply and lay new underfelt fixed to rafters and slate battens to a 150 mm gauge to receive new head nailed slates size 406 × 203 mm to cover a single area of approximately 9 m^2 to the south-east elevation of the single-storey boiler house building.

The above typical clause assumes that all the materials and workmanship involved have been covered by clauses in the preliminaries.

It is possible to extract typical clauses for inclusion in a specification from textbooks, manufacturers' literature and similar sources, but whilst these may well be suitable for most new works it is advisable that specifications for maintenance and adaptation works are individually written to cover the exact conditions, circumstances and requirements of the work involved. This is recommended so that the main objectives of a specification – namely details and clarity – are achieved so that all persons concerned with the works, from the instigator to the operative on site, are fully aware of what is required and how it is to be accomplished. To fully achieve these objectives is not an easy task and students would be well advised to take some typical examples and try writing a specification which is satisfactory in all respects.

Bibliography

Relevant BS – British Standards Institution.
Relevant CP – British Standards Institution.
Relevant Acts, Regulations and Statutory Instruments – HMSO.
DOE Construction Issues 1–30 – HMSO.
Relevant A. J. Handbooks, The Architectural Press.
Relevant information contained in the Barbour Index Library and the
    Barbour Design Library.

Reginald Lee, *Building Maintenance Management*, Crosby Lockwood Staples.
W. A. West, *The Law of Dilapidations*, The Estates Gazette Ltd.
House's Guide to the Construction Industry, House Information Service Ltd.
Cecil C. Handisyde, *Building Materials*, The Architectural Press.
Profitable Building Maintenance, Research and Development Conference
    Papers 1971.
Technology of Building Maintenance, Research and Development Conference
    Papers 1968.
Building Maintenance, Research and Development Committee Report 1972.
A. E. Telling, *Planning Law and Procedure* (5th edn), Butterworth.
Building Management, Gower Press/Industrial Society.
G. Forster, *Building Organization and Procedures*, Longman.
IOB Site Management Information Service Papers, Institute of Building.
IOB Maintenance Information Service Papers, Institute of Building.
W. Atton, *Estimating Applied to Building*, Great Godwin Ltd.
F. Hall, *Building Services and Equipment*, Volume 2, Longman.

164

Index